Challenges for Arabic Machine Translation

Natural Language Processing (NLP)

The scope of NLP ranges from theoretical Computational Linguistics topics to highly practical Language Technology topics. The focus of the series is on new results in NLP and modern alternative theories and methodologies.

For an overview of all books published in this series, please see
http://benjamins.com/catalog/nlp

Volume 9

Challenges for Arabic Machine Translation
Edited by Abdelhadi Soudi, Ali Farghaly, Günter Neumann and Rabih Zbib

Challenges for Arabic Machine Translation

Edited by

Abdelhadi Soudi
École Nationale de l'Industrie Minérale

Ali Farghaly
Monterey Institute of International Studies

Günter Neumann
German Research Center for Artificial Intelligence

Rabih Zbib
BBN Technologies (USA)

John Benjamins Publishing Company
Amsterdam / Philadelphia

The paper used in this publication meets the minimum requirements of the American National Standard for Information Sciences – Permanence of Paper for Printed Library Materials, ANSI Z39.48-1984.

Library of Congress Cataloging-in-Publication Data

Challenges for Arabic machine translation / edited by Abdelhadi Soudi, Ali Farghaly, Günter Neumann and Rabih Zbib.

p. cm. (Natural Language Processing, ISSN 1567-8202 ; v. 9)

Includes bibliographical references and index.

1. Machine translating. 2. English language--Translating into Arabic. 3. Arabic language--Translating into English. 4. Speech processing systems. I. Soudi, Abdelhadi. II. Farghaly, Ali Ahmed Sabry, 1938- III. Neumann, Günter. IV. Zibib, Rabih.

P309.C43 2012

492.7'8020285635--dc23 2012015208

ISBN 978 90 272 4995 1 (Hb ; alk. paper)

ISBN 978 90 272 7362 8 (Eb)

John Benjamins Publishing Co. · P.O. Box 36224 · 1020 ME Amsterdam · The Netherlands

John Benjamins North America · P.O. Box 27519 · Philadelphia PA 19118-0519 · USA

Table of contents

Preface vii

Introduction: Challenges for Arabic machine translation 1
Rabih Zbib & Abdelhadi Soudi

Linguistic resources for Arabic machine translation: The Linguistic Data Consortium (LDC) catalog 15
Ann Bies, Denise DiPersio & Mohamed Maamouri

Using morphology to improve Example-Based Machine Translation: The case of Arabic-to-English translation 23
Violetta Cavalli-Sforza & Aaron B. Phillips

Using semantic equivalents for Arabic-to-English: Example-based translation 49
Kfir Bar & Nachum Dershowitz

Arabic preprocessing for Statistical Machine Translation: Schemes, techniques and combinations 73
Nizar Habash & Fatiha Sadat

Preprocessing for English-to-Arabic Statistical Machine Translation 95
Rabih Zbib & Ibrahim Badr

Lexical syntax for Arabic SMT 109
Hany Hassan

Automatic rule induction in Arabic to English machine translation framework 135
Khaled Shaalan & Ahmad Hany Hossny

Index 155

Preface

Arabic is one of the world's major languages, ranking fifth with respect to the number of native speakers. Yet its presence in language technology research has been limited until recently. Over the last several years, an increasing interest in the Arabic language has given rise to projects targeted at developing fast and accurate Arabic-English Machine Translation and other Arabic Language Technologies applications such as information retrieval, information extraction, and question answering. Several language resources and processing tools for Arabic have been identified and supported during two recent initiatives, namely NEMLAR (Network for Euro-Mediterranean Language Resources, 2003–2005) and MEDAR (Mediterranean Arabic Language and Speech Technology, 2008–2010).

So far, publications on Arabic Language Technology have been spread in various conference proceedings and journals. Some LREC workshops have served as gathering places in the past. For example, "LR & HLT for Semitic Languages" at LREC 2010 in Malta with a collection of papers on Arabic Language Technology, and "HLT & NLP within the Arabic world" at LREC 2008 in Marrakech focused on processing Arabic and local languages of the area.

This book fills a gap in assembling articles about Machine Translation with Arabic as either source or target language. It is a welcome and much-needed repository of important aspects in Arabic Machine Translation such as morphological analysis and syntactic reordering, both central to reducing the distance between Arabic and other languages. The book deserves praise for evading the funding-driven focus on Machine Translation from Arabic to English. Machine Translation in the opposite translation direction is of great practical value to the Arab countries and at the same time a technological challenge because of the morphological richness of the Arabic language. The book permits the comparison of diverging approaches. It is not restricted to the currently dominant paradigm of Statistical Machine Translation but also contains articles on Example-based Machine Translation and a set of arguments why the latter gives advantages for integrating linguistic knowledge.

The editors have succeeded in collecting contributions by the leading figures in the field of Arabic Machine Translation. I am convinced that the book will constitute an important reference point for Arabic Machine Translation and Arabic Language Technology in general.

I sincerely wish that improved Machine Translation systems will facilitate the accessibility of Arabic texts for Western readers and, in reverse, simplify the approachability of English texts for Arabic readers. If our efforts contribute to increased mutual understanding, they are worthwhile.

Martin Volk
Zurich, Switzerland, February 2012

Introduction

Challenges for Arabic machine translation

Rabih Zbib & Abdelhadi Soudi
Raytheon BBN Technologies, Cambridge MA, USA /
Ecole Nationale de l'Industrie Minérale, Rabat, Morocco

1. Overview

Arabic is one of the world's major languages and one of the five official languages of the United Nations. It is the native language of 330 million and is the official language of twenty-two countries used by approximately 260 million people in about twenty countries in North Africa and the Middle East as the primary language for written and oral communication. It is also used as a second language by a further 1.4 billion people in areas including Africa and southeastern Asia. Certainly Arabic poses some unique problems for language technology research. Arabic-speaking countries are characterized by the phenomenon of diglossia: they speak dialects that are traditionally not written and are not always mutually intelligible, but they share a common language known as literary Arabic or Modern Standard Arabic (MSA). Arabic has a complex grammar and morphology, a large degree of ambiguity in word senses, and further ambiguity attributable to a writing system that normally omits diacritics (e.g. short vowels, consonant doubling, inflection marks).

Interest in Arabic is increasing as it gains importance for political, strategic, and business reasons. This interest has given rise to projects targeted at developing fast and accurate Arabic-English Machine Translation (MT). These efforts have been mostly spearheaded by the U.S. Department of Defense, and industrial leaders such as Google or IBM, and a few smaller companies in Europe, United States and Egypt. Many of these efforts have focused on translating from Arabic into English for strategic reasons, but the two directions of translation present some essentially different problems due to the morphological differences (and the degree of specification) of the two languages.

This book collects contributions from the most prominent researchers working on Arabic machine translation today. The contributions in the book span the major paradigms of contemporary machine translation. The empirical, or data-driven, paradigm uses examples of translated sentences in the translation of new sentences, previously unseen by the system. Within the data-driven paradigm, example-based machine translation tries to match the input sentence to example sentences in the corpus; whereas statistical machine translation uses the corpus of translated sentences to estimate parameters of the statistical translation model, then uses that model to translate input sentences. Data-driven translation is typically limited by the quantity and scope of its training data. This is problematic in Arabic due to its complex morphology. If we consider every combination of a stem and morphological affixes to be a separate word, the vocabulary of the training corpus will be quite large. A large vocabulary means that the number of occurrences of each word is quite low.

The other major machine translation paradigm is knowledge-based (or rule-based) machine translation, which is based on the encoding of linguistic knowledge (morphology, syntax, semantics) in the form of deterministic rules, which are used for analysis of the input sentence and translation into the target language.

Many of the proposed data-driven models include little or no explicit linguistic knowledge. However, the boundary between data-driven approaches and rule-based MT approaches is becoming narrower as more and more hybrid systems are being developed.

The need for incorporating linguistic knowledge is a major challenge in Arabic data-driven MT. Recent attempts to build data-driven systems to translate from and to Arabic have demonstrated that the complexity of word and syntactic structure in this language prompts the need for integrating some linguistic knowledge into these MT systems. The issue is, then, how to incorporate this knowledge and with the minimum cost since the amount of linguistic resources added has consequences for computational complexity and portability.

The contributions of this volume show how the unique challenges of Arabic machine translation can be addressed effectively in the context of these MT paradigms

This book is unique in the following ways:

- It is the first volume that focuses on the specific challenges of Arabic machine translation;
- It covers approaches that belong to the three major paradigms of machine translation: Example-based, statistical and knowledge-based;
- It provides broad but rigorous coverage of the methods for incorporating linguistic knowledge into empirical MT (Example-based and Statistical MT);

- Most of the proposed techniques are also applicable to machine translation of Semitic languages other than Arabic, as well as translation of other languages with a complex morphology;
- The book brings together contributions from the most prominent researchers working on Arabic machine translation today, from both academia and industrial research.

We first offer a brief description of the content of the book. Chapter 2 describes Arabic corpora and other linguistic resources developed by the Linguistic Data Consortium (LDC). These resources have had a fundamental role in enabling Arabic machine translation research, including the contributions of this volume. Chapter 3 describes how morphological analysis can be used to enrich translation examples in an example-based machine translation system, as a way to deal with the effect of the complexity of Arabic morphology. In Chapter 4, the use of semantic equivalence is investigated for the same purpose of enriching translation examples. Chapter 5 shows how morphological segmentation can be used in the context of statistical machine translation to address the effect of morphological complexity on machine translation from Arabic. Chapter 6 shows how morphological decomposition can be appropriately modified to improve machine translation from English to Arabic. In the second part of Chapter 6, as well as in Chapter 7, techniques that use syntactic information within the statistical machine translation framework are investigated. Finally, Chapter 8 introduces an approach for learning the translation rules of a transfer-based machine translation system, using the machine learning technique known as Inductive Logic Programming (ILP).

2. Challenges of Arabic machine translation

Machine translation between any two languages is a very challenging problem. Certain aspects of the translation problem, however, become more relevant depending on the linguistic properties of the languages in question. The Arabic language, like other Semitic languages, is characterized by a relatively complex morphology. It has a rich system of morphological inflections. It also affixes certain morphemes, such as prepositions and personal object and possessive pronouns to the word stems. This implies that the equivalent of a whole English sentence can be represented in a single Arabic word. The number of word types in a given Arabic corpus will therefore be larger (usually by 20% to 25%) than the number of word types in a corresponding English corpus of the same size. This morphological complexity presents a challenge to machine translation from Arabic to English or similar languages, which is manifested differently in different MT paradigms. In data-driven machine translation, the challenge is that the Arabic corpus will be sparser than an equivalent English corpus, because the average number of observed instances of a given morphologically complex Arabic token will be lower; and in some cases, the MT system might encounter a new surface form of a word, and not be able to translate it even if it had been trained on data that contains a different morphological form of that word. In the context of knowledge-based machine translation, the challenge presented by the morphological complexity of Arabic is to encode the linguistic knowledge concisely and efficiently, so as to be able to generalize translations to new morphological forms of known words.

As Chapters 3–6 of this volume show, the different machine translation paradigms deal with the issue of complex morphology differently. Example-based machine translation approaches enrich the base of example sentences by over-generating with new morphological forms of the known words, using the morphological analysis of the original example sentences. This allows the MT system to properly translate new morphological forms of known words. Statistical machine translation approaches, on the other hand, use morphological analysis to segment the Arabic side of the data, both at training time and at translation time, into its constituting morphemes. The resulting reduction in the size of the vocabulary implies a reduction in the number of model parameters that need to be learned during the training process, which in turn means the parameters can be estimated more reliably.

The length of Arabic phonemes, both vowels and consonants, is contrastive. Whereas long vowels are written using regular characters, short vowels (a, u, i) are written using small marks called *diacritics,* which are placed above or below the preceding consonant. The doubling of consonant duration, also phonemically contrastive, is marked with a diacritic as well. Diacritics are usually omitted from Arabic text, except in special cases, such as religious text, children's books and language learning material. The absence of diacritics in Arabic text creates an ambiguity in the pronunciation, as well as lexical ambiguity, since two different words, with different (and possibly unrelated) meanings, can share the same non-diacritized spelling. Source ambiguity, a common phenomenon to all human languages, is exacerbated by the lack of diacritics in the case of Arabic. Humans rely on the context and on their knowledge of the lexicon to resolve this ambiguity when reading Arabic text. But this ability is far from being readily available to an automatic machine translation system. Some machine translation systems, especially knowledge-based systems, automatically diacritize the Arabic text as part of the analysis they perform on it. Other systems, including most example-based and statistical systems, deal with lexical ambiguity implicitly. Rather than trying to explicitly resolve the ambiguity, they allow the surrounding context, among other factors, to affect the translation decision.

The remarkable differences between the syntax of Arabic and that of English and other European languages are another source of difficulty for Arabic machine translation. Difference in the structure of the verb phrase, the position of adjectives relative to the nouns they modify, and the marking of definiteness make long distance dependencies in the sentence important for correct translation. Chapters 6 and 7 propose mechanisms for integrating syntactic information into the statistical machine translation framework.

3. Arabic linguistic resources

Both example-based machine translation and statistical machine translation depend on the existence of text corpora. Bilingual corpora of parallel text form the basis for building machine translation systems in these two data-driven paradigms. Monolingual corpora, especially in the target language, are also important for building language models, especially in statistical machine translation. Chapter 2 gives an overview of the Arabic linguistic resources that have been developed by the Linguistic Data Consortium (LDC) over the past two decades. These resources have enabled much of the research in data-driven Arabic natural language processing, and Arabic machine translation, including the work presented in this volume. The corpora listed cover different data types: speech, text, video and lexicons. They also cover different varieties of Arabic: Modern Standard Arabic as well as Egyptian, Gulf and Levantine dialects. Especially relevant to machine translation research have been the corpora of parallel sentences between Arabic and English. LDC has developed large parallel corpora, which have been used for training translation models, as well as data for NIST's Open MT evaluations. The NIST evaluation corpora have become the de facto standard sets for use in research publications on Arabic machine translation. The Penn Arabic Treebank (ATB), a corpus of Arabic sentences with full syntactic trees has also been important for syntax-based Arabic machine translation. The Standard Arabic Morphological Analyzer (SAMA), and its predecessor the Buckwalter Arabic Morphological Analyzer (BAMA), are morphological analysis tools – with supporting lexicons – that determine morphological decompositions of Arabic words. They have had an influential role in the research of morphological methods for Arabic machine translation, including Chapters 3, 4, 5 and 6 of this volume.

4. Example-based machine translation

Chapters 3 and 4 in this book present contributions on improving example-based machine translation from Arabic to English using linguistic information. Example-based machine translation, first proposed by (Nagao 1984), is a data-driven approach to machine translation that attempts to perform translation 'by analogy'. A large corpus of translated example sentences is used to produce a translation for a new sentence. In statistical MT, the corpus of translated sentences is used to create a translation model and associated probabilities at training time, which is then used at run-time (or decoding) to generate translations for new sentences. In example-based MT, on the other hand, the example sentences are used directly to generate the new translations by first matching the input sentence with full example sentences or fragments of sentences, and then composing the matched fragments and adapting them appropriately to produce the translation of the new sentence.

The challenge for example-based machine translation is to expand the set of input sentences that can match the translation in the corpus of examples. When translating from Arabic, the chances of exact matching between the fully inflected surface form of the input and the example sentences are significantly reduced by the morphological complexity of the Arabic source. The chapters in this part present methods on using linguistic analysis of the input to expand the set of input sentences that match the base of translations examples.

Chapter 3 by Cavalli-Sforza and Phillips uses morphological analysis of the Arabic input to improve the quality of example-based Arabic-English machine translation. They propose to generalize from the morphological forms that are observed in the input sentence to new morphological forms using morphological analyses of the input words. They use various heuristics to perform fuzzy matching of morphological features of phrases in the sample input sentences. They show significant improvement in the quality of the translation output, especially with small amounts of example data, where the sparseness problem is more severe. In contrast to over-generation, morphological analysis of Arabic is used within the statistical machine translation paradigm to reduce the sparseness of the data. The Arabic words are segmented into separate morphemes to reduce the size of the Arabic vocabulary and improve the alignments with English.

In Chapter 4, Bar and Dershowitz propose the use of semantic equivalence between Arabic words to expand the space of matching sentences. The effect of using synonyms for nouns and verbs on the performance of an example-based machine translation system is studied. This work also uses morphological information from the Buckwalter Morphological Analyzer to match words at deeper levels of representation, such as the stem and the lemma. The main challenge this chapter addresses is how to determine Arabic synonyms, given that no equivalent of the English *WordNet* exists for Arabic. The authors consider different techniques for extracting synonyms for Arabic nouns and phrases. The first part of the chapter uses noun synonyms. The morphological analysis of the Arabic source is used to define different levels of matching, with associated scores. Noun synonyms are used as an additional feature, and the lack of a reliable Arabic thesaurus is dealt with by using the semantic intersections between the English translations of the Arabic words to define multiple levels of synonymy. The authors suggest that word sense should be used in determining synonym matches, and compensate for the lack of reliable word-sense disambiguation for Arabic by using information about the subject matter of the input sentence. Input sentences are classified using an SVM topic classifier, and synonyms are considered only if their topic sets intersect.

The second part of the chapter uses verb synonyms to increase the possibility of matching between the input sentence and the translation examples. Determining verb synonyms is more challenging because the meaning of an Arabic verb often depends on surrounding prepositions and other particles. The authors present a method for finding longer span equivalences, or *paraphrases*. Using comparable Arabic corpora, the synonyms are found by aligning verb pairs that share the same stem or are deemed to be synonyms, and then looking at the surrounding context in both sentences.

The chapter's experiments use an Arabic-English parallel corpus of news from LDC. They use Arabic news corpora from different sources covering the same time period to find paraphrases of verb phrases. They show an improvement from the use of noun synonyms, especially with a smaller amount of parallel data, where the data sparseness issue is more severe. The techniques of this chapter show a promise for bigger gains when Arabic semantic resources mature and become more available.

One advantage of these methods is that, in principle, they only require morphological and semantic information of Arabic, which makes them readily applicable to translation from Arabic to languages other than English.

5. Statistical machine translation

Statistical machine translation is the most dominant machine translation paradigm, especially in the research community. First suggested in (Brown et al. 1990), it uses supervised machine learning algorithms to learn translation model parameters from a large corpus of parallel sentences. In contrast to example-based machine translation, statistical machine translation does not use the sentence examples directly, but rather uses translation units derived from the data, such as word phrases or hierarchical rules, with corresponding translations and translation probabilities.

A characteristic property of statistical machine translation is its robustness to transformations on the source side. The input to the MT system can undergo any arbitrary transformation as long as the source side of the training data is transformed consistently. It is common to apply such transformations, usually referred to as "preprocessing" steps, to the source side to address issues in the input text, or to reduce differences between the source and target languages. Chapter 5 by Habash and Sadat presents a method for dealing with the morphological complexity of Arabic source and the resulting side effect of data sparseness. Morphologically complex words on the Arabic side are segmented into their constituent morphemes. Naïve pattern matching is not appropriate for detecting the individual morphemes. A deeper morphological analysis is required to determine whether a given sub-word is a morpheme of part of the word stem itself. Habash and Sadat use the morphological analyzer MADA (Habash & Rambow 2005) to perform this analysis. After presenting a thorough description of the issue of morphological complexity in Arabic, the authors propose various segmentation schemes that separate different morpheme classes. They also study how the effect of morphological segmentation varies with size of the training corpus, and find that, in general, the resulting gain is larger with a smaller training size. Their experiments use the Portage phrase-base MT system (Sadat et al. 2005). The Advantages of morphological segmentation for MT are:

i. It reduces the number of unseen words, and reduces the size of the vocabulary. The reduction in the sparseness of the data allows for a more robust estimation of the model parameters.
ii. It improves the quality of Arabic-English word alignments by reducing the gap in the correspondence between the Arabic words and their English translations within the parallel sentence.

In principle, statistical machine translation is symmetric, in that the same corpus of parallel sentences can be used to build a system that translates from A to B or a system that translates from B to A. This flexibility is one of the advantages of the statistical approach. In practice, however, some factors that depend on the translation direction have an effect on the performance of the resulting MT system. Which language the parallel corpus used for training originates in, and which language it was translated into affects the MT output. The training data should preferably originate in the source language of the MT system, since it will be more natural, and will match the characteristics of the machine translation input better. Methods that exploit the special characteristics of the source or target language also break the symmetry of statistical machine translation. They are usually not seamlessly applicable in both directions. The morphological segmentation of Chapter 5 is one such method. When translating from Arabic, the source is segmented consistently before training the MT systems, as well as before translation. When translating to Arabic from another language, segmenting the Arabic side of the training data has the same advantage of reducing the sparseness words on the Arabic side, and improving the quality of the alignments. The problem is that the system will output segmented Arabic, since it is trained on segmented Arabic. In Chapter 6, Zbib and Badr argue for the benefits of morphological segmentation for English-Arabic translation. They explain that the required recombination of the output is not a trivial task, because of morpho-phonological rules that alter the form of the segmented stem word. They suggest rule-based and data-driven methods for reliably recombining the Arabic machine translation output. They also use MADA (Habash & Rambow 2005) for morphological segmentation, and test the recombination methods on a phrase-based statistical machine translation system (Koehn & Hoang 2007). They report consistent gains from using segmentation, especially with small amounts of training data. They find that the best method for recombining the output uses recombination information from the training data, and backs off to using rules based on linguistic knowledge for recombining unseen forms.

In the second part of Chapter 6, the authors address the differences between the syntax of Arabic and that of English. They propose to reorder the English source using predefined syntactic rules that bring the structure of the English sentence closer to that of Arabic. The rules are specified manually, based on systematic difference between the structure of the English noun phrase and verb phrase on the one hand, and their Arabic counterparts on the other. They are applied on the parse tree of the English source before training and then before translation. The authors argue that syntactic reordering is well suited for the Arabic-English translation direction, because the state of statistical parsing for English is more mature and reliable than for other languages.

A limitation of preprocessing methods is that the preprocessing and translation steps are pipelined. The 1-best answer from the preprocessing step is fed as input to the MT system, which implies that the MT system cannot recover from a preprocessing error. An alternative approach is to integrate syntactic or other linguistic information directly into the statistical translation model. The linguistic information contributes 'softly' to the translation model, rather than having to take a 'hard' decision in the preprocessing step. In Chapter 7, Hassan proposes to use syntactic information on the target side to produce more fluent and grammatical output. He notes that using syntactic subtrees that are consistent with the word alignments produces 'redundant syntactic ambiguity', where tree chunks that differ only in their adjuncts are considered separately, and multiple subtrees are associated with the same phrase. This makes it difficult to generalize from training examples. Instead of using full parses, Hassan uses super-tagging using Lexicalized Tree Adjoining Grammars (TAGs) (Bangalore & Joshi 1999), where the syntactic information is represented in a 'supertag' consisting of a TAG fragment that contains POS and sub-categorization information relevant to the lexical entry. Supertagging is a technique of 'almost parsing', which is more flexible than complete parsing, since it produces a supertag sequence for any input phrase. A standard phrase-based statistical MT system is extended using the lexical syntactic descriptions, by using supertags as a feature in the translation model, as well as using an *n-gram* supertag language model.

This approach keeps the advantages of phrase-based statistical MT, with an improved capability for selecting grammatical translations.

The second part of Chapter 7 proposes a more deeply integrated syntactic language model using Combinatory Categorial Grammar (CCG) (Steedman 2000), another lexical syntax formalism. In this case, an incremental parse is dynamically accumulated during decoding. Finally, Hassan presents an extension of the Direct Translation Model (DTM2) that uses syntactic dependency features on the target side.

6. Knowledge-based machine translation

Hybrid approaches to machine translation combine methods from the different MT paradigms, taking advantage of the strength of each. In Chapter 8, Shaalan and Hossny propose to learn translation rules using Inductive Programming Languages (IPL), a machine learning technique that uses logic programming to learn hypotheses from positive and negative examples. They then use the ILP translation model in a deterministic rule-based translation system. They first learn morphological analysis rules using IPL, and also learn transfer rules between word chunks on the Arabic side, and their corresponding English translation. They show that they can learn a considerable number of unique rules from a small amount of parallel sentences, which is one of the main advantages of knowledge-based approaches, compared to corpus-based approaches that require very large parallel corpora.

7. Arabic transliteration scheme

The Habsah-Soudi-Buckwalter transliteration scheme is used in this book (Habash et al. 2007). This scheme is an extension of the Buckwalter transliteration scheme and includes non-ASCII characters whose pronunciation is easier to remember. It is the first easy-to-read and complete one-to-one transliteration of the Arabic script that is consistent with Arabic computer encodings.

Table 1 (Habash et al. 2007: 17–18) below shows the Arabic Transliteration Scheme used in this volume with Examples. The Habash-Soudi-Buckwalter is contrasted with Buckwalter's scheme and a phonological transcription of the examples is also provided.[1]

Table 1. Habsah-Soudi-Buckwalter Arabic transliteration scheme

<table>
<tr><th colspan="3">Characters</th><th colspan="4">Examples</th></tr>
<tr><th>Arabic</th><th>Transliteration</th><th>Buckwalter</th><th>Arabic</th><th>Transliteration</th><th>Transcription</th><th>Gloss</th></tr>
<tr><td>ء</td><td>'</td><td>'</td><td>سماء</td><td>samaA'</td><td>/samā'/</td><td>Sky</td></tr>
<tr><td>آ</td><td>Ā</td><td>|</td><td>آمن</td><td>Āmana</td><td>/'āmana/</td><td>he believed</td></tr>
<tr><td>أ</td><td>Â</td><td>></td><td>سَأل</td><td>saÂala</td><td>/sa'ala/</td><td>he asked</td></tr>
<tr><td>ؤ</td><td>ŵ</td><td>&</td><td>مؤتمر</td><td>muŵtamar</td><td>/mu'tamar/</td><td>Conference</td></tr>
<tr><td>إ</td><td>Ǎ</td><td><</td><td>إنترنت</td><td>Ǎintarnit</td><td>/'intarnit/</td><td>Internet</td></tr>
<tr><td>ئ</td><td>ŷ</td><td>}</td><td>سائل</td><td>saAŷil</td><td>/sā'il/</td><td>Liquid</td></tr>
<tr><td>ا</td><td>A</td><td>A</td><td>كان</td><td>kaAna</td><td>/kāna/</td><td>he was</td></tr>
<tr><td>ب</td><td>b</td><td>b</td><td>بريد</td><td>bariyd</td><td>/barīd/</td><td>mail</td></tr>
<tr><td>ة</td><td>ħ</td><td>p</td><td>مكتبة</td><td>maktabaħ
maktabaħũ</td><td>/maktaba/
/maktabatun/</td><td>library
a library [nom.]</td></tr>
<tr><td>ت</td><td>t</td><td>t</td><td>تنافس</td><td>tanaAfus</td><td>/tanāfus/</td><td>Competition</td></tr>
<tr><td>ث</td><td>Θ</td><td>v</td><td>ثلاثة</td><td>θalaAθaħ</td><td>/θalāθa/</td><td>three</td></tr>
<tr><td>ج</td><td>j</td><td>j</td><td>جميل</td><td>jamiyl</td><td>/jamīl/</td><td>beautiful</td></tr>
<tr><td>ح</td><td>H</td><td>H</td><td>حاد</td><td>HaAd~</td><td>/Hādd/</td><td>Sharp</td></tr>
<tr><td>خ</td><td>x</td><td>x</td><td>خوذة</td><td>xuwðaħ</td><td>/xuwða/</td><td>helmet</td></tr>
<tr><td>د</td><td>d</td><td>d</td><td>دليل</td><td>Daliyl</td><td>/dalīl/</td><td>guide</td></tr>
<tr><td>ذ</td><td>ð</td><td>*</td><td>ذهب</td><td>ðahab</td><td>/ðahab/</td><td>Gold</td></tr>
<tr><td>ر</td><td>r</td><td>r</td><td>رفيع</td><td>Rafiyς</td><td>/rafīς/</td><td>Thin</td></tr>
<tr><td>ز</td><td>z</td><td>z</td><td>زينة</td><td>ziynaħ</td><td>/zīna/</td><td>Decoration</td></tr>
<tr><td>س</td><td>s</td><td>s</td><td>سماء</td><td>samaA'</td><td>/samā'/</td><td>sky</td></tr>
<tr><td>ش</td><td>š</td><td>$</td><td>شريف</td><td>Šariyf</td><td>/šarīf/</td><td>honest</td></tr>
<tr><td>ص</td><td>S</td><td>S</td><td>صوت</td><td>Sawt</td><td>/Sawt/</td><td>Sound</td></tr>
</table>

(*Continued*)

1. cf. (Habash et al. 2007) for the advantages of this transliteration scheme over existing transliteration.

Table 1. Habsah-Soudi-Buckwalter Arabic transliteration scheme (Continued)

Characters			Examples			
Arabic	**Transliteration**	**Buckwalter**	**Arabic**	**Transliteration**	**Transcription**	**Gloss**
ض	D	D	ضرير	Dariyr	/Darīr/	*Blind*
ط	T	T	طويل	Tawiyl	/Tawīl/	*tall*
ظ	Ď	Z	ظلم	Ďulm	/Ďulm/	*injustice*
ع	ς	E	عمل	Σamal	/ςamal/	*Work*
غ	γ	g	غريب	γariyb	/γarīb/	*strange*
ف	f	f	فيلم	Fiylm	/fīlm/	*movie*
ق	q	q	قادر	qaAdir	/qādir/	*capable*
ك	k	k	كريم	kariym	/karīm/	*generous*
ل	l	l	لذيذ	laðiyð	/laðīð/	*delicious*
م	m	m	مدير	mudiyr	/mudīr/	*manager*
ن	n	n	نور	nuwr	/nūr/	*light*
ه	h	h	هول	hawl	/hawl/	*Devastation*
و	w	w	وصل	waSl	/waSl/	*receipt*
ى	ý	Y	على	Σalaý	/ςala/	*On*
ي	y	y	تين	tiyn	/tīn/	*figs*
َ	a	a	دَهَنَ	dahana	/dahana/	*he painted*
ُ	u	u	دُهِنَ	duhina	/duhina/	*It was painted*
ِ	i	i	دُهِنَ	duhina	/duhina/	*It was painted*
ً	ã	F	كتاباً	kitaAbAã	/kitāban/	*A book* [nom.]
ٌ	ũ	N	كتابٌ	kitaAbũ	/kitābun/	*A book* [acc.]
ٍ	ĩ	K	كتابٍ	kitaAbĩ	/kitābin/	*A book* [gen.]
ّ	~	~	كَسَّرَ	kas~ara	/kassara/	*he smashed*
ْ	.	o	مَسْجِد	mas.jid *or* masjid	/masjid/	*mosque*
ـ	_	_	مَســْـجِد	mas.____jid	/masjid/	*mosque*

References

Bangalore, S. and A. Joshi. 1999. Supertagging: An approach to almost parsing. *Computational Linguistics* 25 (2): 237–265.

Brown, P. F., J. Cocke, S. A. Della Pietra, V. J. Della Pietra, F. Jelinek, J. D. Lafferty, R. Mercer, and P. S. Roosin. 1990. A statistical approach to machine translation. *Computational Linguistics* 16 (1): 79–85

Habash, N., and O. Rambow. 2005. Arabic tokenization, part-of speech tagging and morphological disambiguation in one fell swoop. In *Proceedings of the Association for Computational Linguistics* (ACL'05). Ann Arbor MI.

Habash, N., Soudi, A. and T. G. Buckwalter. 2007. Notes on Arabic transliteration. In *Arabic Computational Morphology: Knowledge-based and Empirical Methods. Kluwer/Springer's series on Text, Speech, and Language Technology (series editors Nancy Ide and Jean Veronis)*, Soudi A., Van den Bosch A. and Neumann G (eds).

Koehn, P., and H. Hoang. 2007. Factored translation models. In *Proceedings of EMNLP/CNLL*.

Nagao, M. 1984. A framework of mechanical translation between Japanese and English by analogy principle. In *Artificial and Human Intelligence*, Alick Elithorn & Ranan Banerji (eds), 173–180. Amsterdam: North-Holland.

Sadat, F., H. Johnson, A. Agbago, G. Foster, R. Kuhn, J. Martin, and A. Tikuisis. 2005. Portage: A phrase-based machine translation system. In *Proceedings of the ACL 2005 Workshop on Building and Using Parallel Texts*.

Steedman, M. 2000. *The Syntactic Process*. Cambridge MA: The MIT Press.

Linguistic resources for Arabic machine translation

The Linguistic Data Consortium (LDC) Catalog

Ann Bies, Denise DiPersio & Mohamed Maamouri
Linguistic Data Consortium, University of Pennsylvania

In this chapter, we describe the linguistic resources particularly suitable for Arabic machine translation research and technology development that are published by the Linguistic Data Consortium (LDC). A significant number of the data sets developed by LDC are Arabic language resources, making LDC the leading source for such materials. LDC's Arabic language resources represent all of the data types in LDC's Catalog: speech, text, video and lexicons. Much of this data has already been used for machine translation research, as represented in this volume and throughout the field, and new datasets in the pipeline are expected to benefit machine translation work as well.

1. Introduction

Arabic machine translation research, including the research discussed in the chapters included in this volume, frequently makes use of linguistic resources published by the Linguistic Data Consortium (LDC). In this chapter, we will give an overview of the Arabic language resources at LDC, LDC's distribution model, and some new resources directed at machine translation that will be available in the LDC Catalog in the near future.

The mission of the Linguistic Data Consortium is to support language-related education, research and technology development by creating and sharing language resources including data, tools and standards. Since its founding in 1992, LDC has developed hundreds of corpora in over fifty languages. A significant number of those data sets are Arabic language resources, making LDC the leading source for such materials.

Much of the data developed by LDC has already been used for machine translation research, as represented in this volume and throughout the field, and new datasets in the pipeline are expected to benefit machine translation work as well.

2. LDC's distribution model

LDC is an open consortium of universities, libraries, corporations and government research laboratories who have joined forces to ensure that language resources reach a broad spectrum of users – students, scholars, researchers, developers – in academic, governmental and private organizations. The LDC Catalog contains over 500 holdings and grows at a rate of 30–36 publications annually. This includes resources developed at LDC as well as data sets created by researchers around the world. That data is available to LDC members and nonmembers for use in linguistic research, education and technology development.

LDC's Arabic language resources represent all of the data types found in LDC's Catalog: speech, text, video and lexicons.[1] Those collections particularly suitable for machine translation research and technology development are described below.

3. Arabic speech collections

LDC has designed and executed several studies to create speech corpora for Arabic using a diverse arsenal of microphones and recording technologies. LDC also collects found speech, principally from radio and television broadcast programming. Portions of collected speech are often transcribed, providing the basis for the development of machine translation technologies.

Examples of speech studies in Modern Standard Arabic and selected dialects include:

Arabic Broadcast News Speech LDC2006S46
CALLFRIEND Egyptian Arabic LDC96S49
CALLHOME Egyptian Arabic Speech LDC97S45
CALLHOME Egyptian Arabic Transcripts LDC97T19
Gulf Arabic Conversational Telephone Speech LDC2006S43
Levantine Arabic Speech and Transcripts LDC2005S07, LDC2005S08, LDC2005S14, LDC2005T03, LDC2006S29, LDC2006T07, LDC2007S01, LDC2007S02, LDC2007T01, LDC2007T04
TDT4 Multilingual Broadcast News Speech Corpus LDC2005S11
West Point Arabic Speech LDC2002S02

1. To access LDC's Catalog and for further information, please see the LDC website at www.ldc.upenn.edu.

4. Arabic text collections

LDC collects large amounts of Arabic text from a variety of sources including newswire and web text (blogs, newsgroups, email) in various domains. Two groups of corpora developed from that material are particularly suited for machine translation applications: parallel text corpora and the series of corpora used in NIST's (US National Institute of Standards and Technology) Open Machine Translation (OpenMT) technology evaluations.

4.1 Parallel text

LDC creates translations for large volumes of Arabic newswire, broadcast transcripts and weblog and newsgroup text. Most translations are performed by humans and undergo a series of rigorous quality checks. Other parallel text data sets are automatically generated. The resulting parallel corpora (principally Arabic to English) provide training material for machine translation systems. Examples include the following:

GALE Phase 1 Arabic Broadcast News Parallel Text – Part 1 LDC2007T24
GALE Phase 1 Arabic Blog Parallel Text LDC2008T02
GALE Phase 1 Arabic Newsgroup Parallel Text – Parts 1 and 2 LDC2009T03, LDC2009T09
ISI Arabic-English Automatically Extracted Parallel Text LDC2007T08
Multiple-Translation Arabic (MTA) Parts 1 and 2 LDC2003T18, LDC2005T05

4.2 NIST resources

LDC's Catalog includes resources from each of NIST's OpenMT evaluation campaigns. These are designed as turnkey packages: they contain the source data, reference translations and scoring software used in the evaluation that can then be utilized to replicate the tests and evaluate in-house machine translation systems. The Arabic source data in these evaluations was typically newswire, broadcast and/or web material.

Examples of corpora containing Arabic materials include the following:

NIST 2002 Open Machine Translation (OpenMT) Evaluation LDC2010T10
NIST 2003 Open Machine Translation (OpenMT) Evaluation LDC2010T11
NIST 2004 Open Machine Translation (OpenMT) Evaluation LDC2010T12
NIST 2005 Open Machine Translation (OpenMT) Evaluation LDC2010T14
NIST 2006 Open Machine Translation (OpenMT) Evaluation LDC2010T17
NIST 2008 Open Machine Translation (OpenMT) Evaluation LDC2010T21
NIST 2009 Open Machine Translation (OpenMT) Evaluation LDC2010T23

5. Arabic morphological analyzer

The LDC Standard Arabic Morphological Analyzer (SAMA) Version 3.1 is based on, and updates, the Buckwalter Arabic Morphological Analyzer (BAMA) 2.0, which was developed by Tim Buckwalter (Buckwalter 2004) and used in several of the following chapters in this volume.

SAMA 3.1 is a software tool for the morphological analysis of Standard Arabic. SAMA 3.1 considers each Arabic word token in all possible 'prefix-stem-suffix' segmentations, and lists all known/possible annotation solutions, with assignment of all diacritic marks, morpheme boundaries (separating clitics and inflectional morphemes from stems), and all Part-of-Speech (POS) labels and glosses for each morpheme segment.

The input format, output format, and data layer of SAMA 3.1 were designed to be backward compatible with BAMA. Incremental changes to the data layer in SAMA have resulted in:

- increased lexicon coverage in the dictionary files
- important changes and additions to the inventory of POS tags
- more possible solutions generated for numerous word forms

The structure of the dictionary and morphotactic tables has remained the same (the tables provided with SAMA 3.1 differ from the BAMA 2.0 tables only in size and content, not in format). Logical separation between the software layer and data layer allows the new software tools to be used with previous versions of the tables. UTF-8 is the default input/output and internal character encoding for SAMA 3.1, with automatic conversion of different input encodings (cp1256, iso-8859-6, and Buckwalter transliteration are also accepted). With this change, the use of UTF-8 as input is now fully supported, eliminating a range of problems that would result from having to convert to cp1256 for analysis.

The LDC Catalog references for BAMA 2.0 and SAMA 3.1 are as follows:

> Buckwalter Arabic Morphological Analyzer Version 2.0 LDC2004L02
> LDC Standard Arabic Morphological Analyzer (SAMA) Version 3.1 LDC2010L01

6. Arabic treebank and parallel English treebank

Arabic treebanks and parallel English treebanks are frequently crucial to developing parsing and machine translation systems, including several systems discussed in this volume. Treebanks are fully parsed corpora that are manually annotated for syntactic structure at the sentence level and for POS or morphological information at the token level. Treebanks are widely used in the Natural Language Processing (NLP) community to support the creation and training of parsers and taggers, work on machine translation and speech recognition, and research on joint syntactic and semantic role labeling. Treebanks have also been used as the basis for downstream annotation projects which have also been used in machine translation work, such as PropBanks, the Penn Discourse Treebank and word alignment. LDC produces both Arabic and parallel English treebanks in house, as well as publishing externally produced resources such as the Prague Arabic Dependency Treebank.

The Penn Arabic Treebank (ATB) project began in 2001 at LDC. ATB corpora are annotated for morphological information, POS and English gloss, all at the token level, and for syntactic structure in a style similar to Penn Treebank II (Bies et al. 1995). LDC takes advantage of a pragmatic mixture of manual, semi-automatic and fully automatic annotation methods (Maamouri et al. 2004; Maamouri et al. 2009; Maamouri & Bies 2010).

Improved annotation guidelines, increased inter-annotator agreement and continued improvement in parsing scores are the result of a fruitful collaboration between data producers, sponsors and end users (Maamouri et al. 2008; Kulick et al. 2010; Maamouri et al. 2011). It is expected that continued collaboration will benefit both annotation production and future NLP applications. Current Arabic Treebank guidelines can be found at projects.ldc.upenn.edu/ArabicTreebank. Current English Treebank guidelines can be found at projects.ldc.upenn.edu/gale/task_specifications/EnglishXBank.

ATB annotation is in the process of expanding its genre coverage from the newswire text genre to include also Arabic dialects and Arabic speech and web corpora, along with parallel English data, to support the development of dialect parsers, speech recognition and machine translation efforts (Maamouri et al. 2010). The volumes and genres of Arabic Treebank that have been produced at LDC as of December 2011 are shown in Table 1.

Table 1. Arabic Treebank genres and volumes produced at LDC as of December 2011

Genre	Tree tokens
Newswire Text	750K
Broadcast News	530K
Broadcast Conversation	200K
Web Text	250K
Dialectal Broadcast Conversation	150K

Table 2 shows the volumes and genres of LDC English Treebank for data that is translated from (and parallel to) the corresponding ATB data.

Table 2. English Treebank genres and volumes (which are parallel to LDC Arabic Treebank) produced at LDC as of December 2011

Genre	Tree tokens
Newswire Text	553K
Broadcast News	500K
Broadcast Conversation	150K
Web Text	157K
Dialectal Broadcast Conversation	250K

Due to the multiple levels of annotation inherent in the treebank process and the desire to distribute the annotated data as needed by the community, many treebank corpora in the LDC Catalog have several versions. Each successive version of annotation on the same data set is given a new version number (thus, v2.0 supercedes v1.0, etc.). Only the most up-to-date version of each corpus is listed here. The "Part" numbers refer to specific data sets and are not cumulative (thus, Part 3 is a dataset entirely independent of Part 1, etc.).

Much of the updated Arabic Treebank newswire data has been published in the LDC Catalog already. The intention is to publish the English Treebanks parallel to Arabic Treebank as well as the new genres in the LDC Catalog in 2012. The most up-to-date Arabic Treebank and parallel English Treebank resources that are currently in the LDC Catalog are as follows:

Arabic Treebank: Part 1 v 4.1 LDC2010T13
Arabic Treebank: Part 2 v 3.1 LDC2011T09
Arabic Treebank: Part 3 v 3.2 LDC2010T08
Arabic Treebank: Part 4 v 1.0 (MPG Annotation) LDC2005T30
Prague Arabic Dependency Treebank 1.0 LDC2004T23
English-Arabic Treebank v 1.0 LDC2006T10
English Translation Treebank: An-Nahar Newswire LDC2012T02

7. Arabic-English word alignment

Arabic-English word alignment resources were developed at LDC with machine translation specifically in mind. Word alignment indicates corresponding word relations in parallel text, usually text in a source language and a translation into the target language (Li et al. 2011). Word alignment is performed on segmented sentences, which may be either treebanked or not treebanked. The treebanked and aligned corpora, known as parallel aligned treebanks (PATs), show promise as a resource for improving machine translation technology, and thus there has recently been an increasing demand for such data. LDC and its academic partners have been developing PATs such as Arabic-English for several years. The Arabic-English PATs are parallel Arabic and English treebanks annotated with morphological and syntactic structures that are aligned at sentence as well as sub-sentence levels. Treebank annotations for the Arabic-English PAT are taken from the Penn Arabic Treebank (ATB) and its corresponding parallel English Treebank (EATB). The final PAT corpora are created with an infrastructure that integrates existing parallel treebank annotations through two levels of alignment with corpus-wide data mapping and indexing. These resources are discussed in Li et al. (2010) and Grimes et al. (2010).

LDC has word aligned approximately 2.2 million words of Arabic-English data (including both treebank and non-treebank sources), and out of that total, approximately 400,000 words are parallel aligned treebank. The intention is to publish this data in the LDC Catalog in 2012.

8. Additional resources

There are a variety of Arabic resources at LDC that do not fit into the above categories but might be of use to researchers in machine translation. Among others, these include the OntoNotes corpora and the Egyptian Colloquial Arabic Lexicon.

The OntoNotes project includes Arabic PropBank, word sense, coreference and name annotation. The advantages of parallel PropBanks and semantic role labeling for machine translation have been suggested in Wu et al. (2010) and Lo & Wu (2010). OntoNotes publication versions are cumulative (thus, v4.0 includes the data in v3.0, etc.).

The Egyptian Colloquial Arabic Lexicon represents the first electronic pronunciation dictionary of Egyptian Colloquial Arabic, the spoken variety of Arabic found in Egypt. The dialect of Egyptian Colloquial Arabic provided in this dictionary is Cairene Arabic. This lexicon has informed machine translation work such as Salloum & Habash (2011).

Examples of additional Arabic resources in the LDC Catalog include the following:

OntoNotes Release 4.0 LDC2011T03
Egyptian Colloquial Arabic Lexicon LDC99L22

References

Bies, A., M. Ferguson, K. Katz, and R. MacIntyre. 1995. *Bracketing Guidelines for Treebank II Style*. Penn Treebank Project, University of Pennsylvania, CIS Technical Report MS-CIS-95-06.

Buckwalter, T. 2004. Issues in Arabic orthography and morphological analysis. In *Proceedings of the Workshop on Computational Approaches to Arabic Script-based Languages.*

Grimes, S., X. Li, A. Bies, S. Kulick, X. Ma, and S. Strassel. 2010. Creating Arabic-English parallel word-aligned treebank corpora at LDC. In *Proceedings of the LREC 2010 Workshop on Language Resources and Human Language Technologies for Semitic Languages.*

Kulick, S., A. Bies, and M. Maamouri. 2010. Consistent and flexible integration of morphological annotation in the Arabic Treebank. In *Proceedings of the Seventh International Conference on Language Resources and Evaluation.*

Li, X., X. Ma, S. Grimes, S. Strassel, G. Krug, and D. Zakhary. 2011. In *Handbook of Natural Language Processing and Machine Translation: DARPA Global Autonomous Language Exploitation*, Joseph Olive, Caitlin Christianson & John McCary (eds). Berlin: Springer.

Li, X., S. Strassel, S. Grimes, S. Ismael, X. Ma, N. Ge, A. Bies, N. Xue, and M. Maamouri. 2010. Parallel aligned treebank corpora at LDC: Methodology, annotation and integration. In *Proceedings of the Workshop on Annotation and Exploitation of Parallel Corpora (AEPC).*

Lo, C., and D. Wu. 2010. Evaluating machine translation utility via semantic role labels. In *Proceedings of the Seventh International Conference on Language Resources and Evaluation.*

Maamouri, M., and A. Bies. 2010. The Penn Arabic Treebank. In *Arabic Computational Linguistics* [CSLI Studies in Computational Linguistics], Ali Farghaly (ed.), 103–135. Stanford CA: CSLI.

Maamouri, M., A. Bies, T. Buckwalter, and W. Mekki. 2004. The Penn Arabic Treebank: Building a large-scale annotated Arabic corpus. In *Proceedings of NEMLAR 2004.*

Maamouri, M., A. Bies, and S. Kulick. 2008. Enhancing the Arabic Treebank: A collaborative effort toward new annotation guidelines. In *Proceedings of the Sixth International Conference on Language Resources and Evaluation.*

Maamouri, M., A. Bies, and S. Kulick. 2009. Creating a methodology for Large-scale correction of treebank annotation: The case of the Arabic Treebank. In *Proceedings of MEDAR 2nd International Conference on Arabic Language Resources and Tools.*

Maamouri, M., A. Bies, and S. Kulick. 2011. Upgrading and enhancing the Penn Arabic Treebank: A GALE challenge. In *Handbook of Natural Language Processing and Machine Translation: DARPA Global Autonomous Language Exploitation*, Joseph Olive, Caitlin Christianson & John McCary (eds). Berlin: Springer.

Maamouri, M., A. Bies, S. Kulick, W. Zaghouani, D. Graff, and M. Ciul. 2010. From speech to trees: Applying treebank annotation to Arabic broadcast news. In *Proceedings of the Seventh International Conference on Language Resources and Evaluation.*

Salloum, W., and N. Habash. 2011. Dialectal to standard Arabic paraphrasing to improve Arabic-English statistical machine translation. In *Proceedings of EMNLP 2011, Conference on Empirical Methods in Natural Language Processing.*

Wu, S., J. D. Choi, and M. Palmer. 2010. Detecting cross-lingual semantic similarity using parallel propbanks. In *Proceedings of the Ninth Conference of the Association for Machine Translation in the Americas.*

Using morphology to improve Example-Based Machine Translation

The case of Arabic-to-English translation

Violetta Cavalli-Sforza & Aaron B. Phillips
School of Science and Engineering, Al Akhawayn University, Ifrane, Morocco / Language Technologies Institute Carnegie Mellon University, Pittsburgh, Pennsylvania

We describe how morphological information was used in an Example-Based Arabic-to-English Machine Translation system to produce significant improvement in translation quality on both small and large corpora. We experimented with different methods of generalizing morphology to obtain more candidate source-side matches, while retaining information about the specific input to be translated. This information was then used with adaptation rules and a language model to generate context-appropriate target-side fragments, select and combine them. We outline essential differences between Statistical MT (SMT) and Example-based MT (EBMT), compare ourselves to other EBMT systems used with morphologically complex languages, and justify our choice of EBMT over SMT.

1. Introduction

This chapter, jointly with Bar and Dershowitz's contribution (Chapter 4), distinguishes itself from others in this book by describing work on Arabic-to-English Example-Based Machine Translation (EBMT), instead of Statistical Machine Translation (SMT). The choice of EBMT raises questions concerning differences between approaches and the reasons for preferring the example-based over the more mainstream statistical approach. While there are key differences between the two, there are also similarities. Moreover, in response to problems that are not handled well by any one approach, the field of MT has often adopted a hybridization strategy, causing the boundaries between EBMT and SMT to blur. Finally, within the wide range of EBMT variations, our approach falls very much on the statistical end of the spectrum.

The research presented in this chapter is relevant to empirical approaches in general because it addresses a weakness shared by all such approaches: they are typically limited by the quantity and scope of their training data, a problem specifically for Arabic and other morphologically complex languages. To have data for every possible surface realization of a word in context requires a large training corpus vocabulary. This, in turn, means that the number of occurrences of each word is quite low and even a reasonably large corpus will not cover everything we want to translate, whereas translation accuracy is enhanced when many examples of the same text are available. Our work addresses specifically this issue: we aim to transform the input to be translated into a more general class whose membership includes larger portions of the training corpus, so that the system has more examples from which to choose the best translation. This strategy increases the coverage of the available examples and captures things that are not directly seen in the text. Even if an exact translation cannot be found in the corpus, a generalized translation can still be largely correct and is superior to no translation at all.

We start by introducing EBMT in general, distinguishing it from SMT, and motivating our choice of approach. We then describe briefly our specific EBMT system before focusing on the specific details of our approach and the results obtained. Before concluding, we consider how other EBMT systems have dealt with morphologically complex languages.

2. Example-Based Machine Translation: What is it and why use it?

EBMT is a form of automated translation that, like SMT, is data-driven: it uses a large corpus of previously-translated example sentences to create a translation for a new sentence. As aptly discussed by Carl and Way (2003: xvii-xxxi), there are many approaches to EBMT, each making different assumptions about the steps, processes, techniques and representations used. As a result, EBMT systems share some characteristics with both Rule-Based Machine Translation (RBMT) systems and SMT, without being one or the other. For example, although EBMT does not use rules to perform translation, rule-like structures may be used to select the examples or to adapt the translation once obtained from the corpus; translation patterns, either hand-coded or automatically learned from the parallel corpus, may be considered rules directing translation in specific ways. Similarly, EBMT systems may use statistical methods in some subset of their operations, though they do so differently than SMT systems.

SMT systems have undergone significant evolution, modification and enrichment since the first system developed at IBM T.J. Watson Labs (Brown et al. 1990) and have incorporated different doses of linguistic knowledge. However, they usually make the same training-time versus run-time distinction. At training-time, a translation model is learned from an (ideally) sentence aligned bilingual corpus through unsupervised learning techniques; a language model is computed from a monolingual corpus of the target language. Both are essentially built by estimating the statistical parameters of a complex mathematical model. At run-time the best translation is searched for by maximizing the probability considering the two models. The corpus is not present at run-time and the translation is computed from very large probability tables.

In contrast, in EBMT systems, the corpus is always present at run-time. EBMT follows a matching and recombination approach. The two major steps in obtaining a translation for a given text to be translated are: (1) finding and selecting matching source-side examples, either full sentences or fragments of a sentence, in the bilingual sentence-aligned corpus; (2) replacing, modifying, or adapting fragment(s) to generate the translation. These operations may be rule-driven or data-driven, but the mapping of a source segment into a target sentence is largely guided by translation examples. Candidate translation fragments may be stitched together at run-time with the help of a target language model like those used in SMT. The 'training' performed in an EBMT system may include operations such as indexing the corpus, pre-computing alignments and learning generalized translation patterns. These steps are performed once, before run-time, to avoid repeating work and achieve better runtime performance.

Why did we choose EBMT for our work instead of the apparently 'main-stream' SMT approach? The primary reason was that we wanted to investigate the linguistic idea of over-generating example matches and filtering later, which could be implemented more easily in EBMT since the filtering component of our approach required us to have the full corpus plus annotations available at run-time. One of the key points of our work is being able to find phrases we have not seen with that particular surface realization, though this results in overgeneralized matches. We then apply techniques to the matched examples to select those that fit best, and adapt them to the context of occurrence. In SMT the input is not known at training time and the corpus is not present at runtime so, although theoretically we could model all possible phrases we might see, this would not be practical. Since we use the runtime input to search examples, EBMT is a better fit for our approach.

While EBMT was clearly the right data-driven machine translation framework within which to experiment with our approach, there are other reasons why one might choose EBMT over SMT. First, we can argue that EBMT, in its basic conception, is more intuitive and resembles how human beings learn languages and perform translation. Instead of relying on complex mathematical models as does SMT, EBMT finds similar examples and changes the associated translation as necessary to fit the situation at hand. Studying examples is also how we often learn to produce sentences in a foreign language: to obtain full control of a language, we must learn vocabulary and rules, but simple production and adaptation of sentence fragments can go a long way towards effective communication (Zimmer 2010). Similarly, some have remarked that professional translators tend to translate by "chunks" (Somers 2003: 5–7) rather than word by word. Translation memory systems, in which full sentences are matched with some degree of fuzziness to provide initial translations, have become widely used in the translation industry.

Second, an argument in support of EBMT is that it usually performs better than SMT when little data is available; EBMT predates SMT as a data-driven approach, partially because of this very reason. The idea of EBMT was purportedly developed in the 1970s at Brigham Young University, presented officially in 1981 (Somers 2003: 6), and published in 1984 (Nagao 1984). It preceded by a few years the first SMT system (Brown et al. 1990), based on the Hansard corpus (Roukos et al. 1995), the first large scale publicly available parallel corpus. SMT systems require large parallel corpora in order to estimate accurately the parameters of the underlying statistical models and, to the extent that larger corpora mean more language coverage, the larger the better Callison-Burch (2007). EBMT systems have initially been built with significantly smaller corpora, touting as one of their assets the ability to improve quality of translation incrementally by adding corpus (e.g. Brown 1996).

The final reason for choosing EBMT might just be that there is no reason for everybody to pursue a single MT approach. While EBMT has not been a popular approach in the United States – the only research group working with that approach was indeed ours – it has received substantially more attention in Europe and Japan, among other places. In fact, it is a little misleading to say that SMT is the mainstream approach. MT conferences programs for the last few years show the use of multiple approaches, ranging from Knowledge-Based MT to EBMT (including translation memories), to SMT. Moreover, these days few systems can claim to be purely one type or the other. Most are hybrid systems, combining different approaches to perform distinct tasks. In a few cases, multi-engine systems, like the Pangloss-lite framework (Frederking & Brown 1996) are used. These use multiple translation engines, selecting and/or combining their output in a final step prior to outputting the best translation(s).

3. Adding morphology to EBMT for Arabic-to-English translation

We turn our attention now to the core topic of this chapter, how morphology can be used to improve EBMT for Arabic to English translation. We reiterate the data sparseness challenge faced by data-driven systems in general, and in translating from Arabic in particular. Bar & Dershowitz (Chapter 4) reproduce for Arabic the results previously obtained for Spanish by Callison-Burch (2007): while the percentage of word sequences (*n*-grams) covered increases with corpus size, even with very large corpora most sequences longer than one word remain uncovered. The complex morphology of Arabic, which gives rise to many surface forms for a single word, exacerbates data sparseness.

Given that a morphologically exact match cannot be guaranteed even in a large corpus, it makes sense to generalize away some features of the word in order to find matches, even if inexact ones. Having a choice of several matches, improves the chances of finding a decent though (morphologically) imperfect translation, even more when the target language, English for example, has a relatively poor inflectional morphology. Although the morphological details of the source word may have been generalized away, the translation is often safe because the same English word covers several inflected variants of the Arabic word. In addition, the translation is likely to be understandable even if it is ungrammatical.

However, morphological generalization is only part of the challenge. Due to the lack of diacritic signs in most text and the ambiguity in analysis the missing information engenders, the exact identification of an Arabic word presents extra difficulty. On one hand, the presence of inflectional and derivational affixes can be seen as limiting the possible analyses, because certain affixes can only occur with certain parts of speech and are subject to some phonological constraints. On the other hand, the presence of the affixes can make a sequence of characters look like altogether different words derived from different roots or stems and with very different meanings, as well as different inflectional variants of the same basic lexical entry. For example, by looking at the word out of context, it is impossible to distinguish between different parts of speech (e.g. علم *çlm* can be عِلْم *çilom* 'knowledge' – a noun – or عَلَّمَ *çal~ama* "he taught, instructed, imparted knowledge" – a verb – among other possibilities) and different derivational forms (e.g. different measures of a verb). When considering all the ways in which a given Arabic token can be analyzed, it is very easy to overgeneralize or generalize incorrectly and produce invalid translations.

We begin by reviewing how ambiguity and the morphological analyses of words impact generalization, then we trace through the development of our approach looking at two successive phases of the work. The first phase, reported in (Phillips & Cavalli-Sforza 2006), was strictly concerned with two issues: (1) **generalization**, in order to increase the number of potential matches for the input to be translated; and (2) **filtering**, to limit overgeneralization. In the second phase (Phillips, Cavalli-Sforza & Brown 2007), a more sophisticated generalization mechanism was developed, and filtering was augmented with **adaptation** to provide better quality translations from the generalized matches.

3.1 Generalization and morphological analysis in BAMA

We based our generalizations on the output of the widely-used Buckwalter Arabic Morphological Analyzer (BAMA) (Buckwalter 2004), a context-insensitive morphological analyzer that identifies all possible combinations of stems and affixes for a word (annotated with the morphological features they represent), without indicating the likelihood of each combination. Multiple analyses arise not only as a result of missing diacritic markings but also due to orthographical variations (e.g. writing ي as ى), and errors. Table 1, on the next page, gives an example of all the various morphological parses for the word وكالة *wkAlħ* 'agency'.

Table 1. Possible analyses of the word وكالة *wkAlħ* 'agency'

Stem	LemmaID	Analysis[1]
wkAl	wikAlap_1	wikAl/NOUN ap/NSUFF_FEM_SG
wkAl	wikAlap_1	wikAl/NOUN ap/NSUFF_FEM_SG+u/CASE_DEF_NOM
wkAl	wikAlap_1	wikAl/NOUN ap/NSUFF_FEM_SG+a/CASE_DEF_ACC
wkAl	wikAlap_1	wikAl/NOUN ap/NSUFF_FEM_SG+i/CASE_DEF_GEN
wkAl	wikAlap_1	wikAl/NOUN ap/NSUFF_FEM_SG+N/CASE_INDEF_NOM
wkAl	wikAlap_1	wikAl/NOUN ap/NSUFF_FEM_SG+F/CASE_INDEF_ACC
wkAl	wikAlap_1	wikAl/NOUN ap/NSUFF_FEM_SG+K/CASE_INDEF_GEN
wkAl	wikAlap_1	wakAl/NOUN ap/NSUFF_FEM_SG
wkAl	wikAlap_1	wakAl/NOUN ap/NSUFF_FEM_SG+u/CASE_DEF_NOM
wkAl	wikAlap_1	wakAl/NOUN ap/NSUFF_FEM_SG+a/CASE_DEF_ACC
wkAl	wikAlap_1	wakAl/NOUN ap/NSUFF_FEM_SG+i/CASE_DEF_GEN
wkAl	wikAlap_1	wakAl/NOUN ap/NSUFF_FEM_SG+N/CASE_INDEF_NOM
wkAl	wikAlap_1	wakAl/NOUN ap/NSUFF_FEM_SG+F/CASE_INDEF_ACC
wkAl	wikAlap_1	wakAl/NOUN ap/NSUFF_FEM_SG+K/CASE_INDEF_GEN
wkAl	wikAlap_2	wikAl/NOUN ap/NSUFF_FEM_SG
wkAl	wikAlap_2	wikAl/NOUN ap/NSUFF_FEM_SG+u/CASE_DEF_NOM
wkAl	wikAlap_2	wikAl/NOUN ap/NSUFF_FEM_SG+a/CASE_DEF_ACC
wkAl	wikAlap_2	wikAl/NOUN ap/NSUFF_FEM_SG+i/CASE_DEF_GEN
wkAl	wikAlap_2	wikAl/NOUN ap/NSUFF_FEM_SG+N/CASE_INDEF_NOM
wkAl	wikAlap_2	wikAl/NOUN ap/NSUFF_FEM_SG+F/CASE_INDEF_ACC
wkAl	wikAlap_2	wikAl/NOUN ap/NSUFF_FEM_SG+K/CASE_INDEF_GEN
kAl	kAl~_1	wa/CONJ kAl~/ADJ ap/NSUFF_FEM_SG

(*Continued*)

1. The transliteration used in the Analysis is the one that appears in the BAMA output.

Table 1. (Continued)

Stem	LemmaID	Analysis[1]
kAl	kAl~_1	wa/CONJ kAl~/ADJ ap/NSUFF_FEM_SG+u/CASE_DEF_NOM
kAl	kAl~_1	wa/CONJ kAl~/ADJ ap/NSUFF_FEM_SG+a/CASE_DEF_ACC
kAl	kAl~_1	wa/CONJ kAl~/ADJ ap/NSUFF_FEM_SG+i/CASE_DEF_GEN
kAl	kAl~_1	wa/CONJ kAl~/ADJ ap/NSUFF_FEM_SG+N/CASE_INDEF_NOM
kAl	kAl~_1	wa/CONJ kAl~/ADJ ap/NSUFF_FEM_SG+F/CASE_INDEF_ACC
kAl	kAl~_1	wa/CONJ kAl~/ADJ ap/NSUFF_FEM_SG+K/CASE_INDEF_GEN
Al	|lap_1	wa/CONJ+ka/PREP |l/NOUN ap/NSUFF_FEM_SG
Al	|lap_1	wa/CONJ+ka/PREP |l/NOUN ap/NSUFF_FEM_SG+i/CASE_DEF_GEN
Al	|lap_1	wa/CONJ+ka/PREP |l/NOUN ap/NSUFF_FEM_SG+K/CASE_INDEF_GEN

The morphological generalization technique we adopted aimed to find examples in the training corpus that match the Arabic source text ignoring morphological inflection. We generalized every word in the corpus (retaining information about its original form and passing it along as 'metadata') and replaced the surface form of each word with a token that is the same across all morphological inflections. But what token could we use for each word that was sufficient for our purposes?

The meaning of most Arabic words is contained within the stem, which BAMA returns; however, words with multiple analyses may cover multiple stems, so the stem was not sufficiently general for our purposes. Each stem in BAMA is also associated with a 'lemmaID', which provides slightly more sophisticated means of generalizing. The lemmaID roughly indicates the sense of the word: it groups together a fairly small set of words that are derived from the same root, share similar stems, and have similar meanings; it also provides English glosses. For example, both the singular (كِتَاب *kitAb*) and plural (كُتُب *kutub*) stems for the word 'book' would be grouped under the same lemmaID. On the other hand, not all stems derived from the same root will be grouped under the same lemmaID. For example the stems كَتَب *katab* تَكَاتَب *takAtab* are derived from the same root ك- ت- ب *k-t-b* and intersect with different patterns to give distinct meanings – "to write" and "to correspond" respectively – and are therefore associated with different lemmaIDs.[2]

2. Using the root would yield even more generalization but many words that share a root are only vaguely related. Initial experiments did not support following this approach.

Generally, a human can determine the correct word by the meaning and context of a sentence. Though there are analyzers that look at the surrounding context and select the most likely analysis (Habash & Rambow 2005), we preferred to delay such decisions to avoid potentially removing good candidates and allow the system to select the best analysis at runtime.[3] Not requiring a more advanced analyzer makes the system's requirements modest and the transition to another language much easier. However, without a more sophisticated morphological analyzer, we cannot strip the affixes because we do not always know which part of the word is the stem. Even if we could identify the stem, that is not always good enough because it may change form. Thus we needed a level of abstraction higher than the stem and even higher than the lemmaID.[4]

3.2 Phase 1: Focus on generalization and filtering

The first phase of our research focused on experimenting with alternative techniques for generalizing across morphological variants and analyses. Generalization was performed by preprocessing both the corpus and the input to be translated. We used the output of a morphological analyzer to reduce the Arabic words in different ways and then attached metadata with the original form of the word; the metadata was used at runtime by a filtering process to reduce the amount of overgeneralization.

3.2.1 *Generalization*

The first issue that arose was how to choose among multiple analyses. With a large corpus of hand-analyzed Arabic text, we could choose the stem based on its frequency of occurrence and generalize by picking that stem to represent the generalized word. Lacking that, the only information we can use from BAMA is which stem gives the most analyses, though it is not guaranteed to be the most frequent stem in natural text. For example, the analysis of the word وكالة *wkAlħ* 'agency', as shown in Table 1, has three possible stems: *wkAl*, *kAl*, and *Al*. Of these, *wkAl* is used 21 times, *kAl* is used 7 times, and *Al* is only used 3 times. Using the most common stem in the analyses, we select *wkAl* as the canonical stem for the word *wkAlħ*. This initial approach to generalization had reasonable impact, showing a 5% increase in the number of words covered by an *n*-gram (*n* word sequence) with $n \geq 4$. We used *n*-gram matches as a measure of performance because word sequences are the raw material out of which corpus-based systems construct their

3. Preliminary experiments with early ambiguity removal showed worse performance.

4. Our system is not dependent on BAMA, but if stems can change form (as they do in Arabic) then the analyzer must provide some canonical form for the stem.

translations. Longer fragments matches are preferred to shorter ones (including single words) because matching a larger context on the source side is likely to produce more accurate and smoother translations on the target side.

LemmaIDs are typically more general than just the stemmed word because they can encapsulate multiple stems. If we use the most frequent lemmaID instead of the most frequent stem, for the word وكالة *wkAlħ* 'agency' we would select the lemmaID 'wikAlap_1', which spans the stems wik*Al* and *wakAl* (the same stem if vowels are removed). Generalizing words by the most frequent lemmaID performed better than using the most frequent stem from the BAMA analysis, but only increased coverage of phrases of n-gram with $n \geq 4$ by 2%. Since a given surface form can be subsumed by several lemmaIDs, even the lemmaID is not really general enough.

The next step towards greater generalization was to try clustering the stems so as to have each stem map to a single generalized token and all possible stems for any given word to map to the same generalized token. In this method of clustering, if two words share any possible analyses (in terms of the smallest unit we are looking at, e.g. stems) then we declare that they are in the same cluster. Given the analyses in Table 2 below, we cluster حجمي *Hjmy* and أحجم *ÂHjm* together in one cluster and قاسمي *qAsmy* and تقاسم *tqAsm* together in another cluster. These words are clustered together because they share at least one stem, though the shared stems may belong to different lemmaIDs. For example, the surface form *Hjmy* can be from stem *Hjmy* 'volumetric' (lemmaID 'Hajomiy~_1'), or stem *Hjm* "volume, size" (lemmaID 'Hajom_1'). The stem *Hjm* (present/imperfect) is also is associated with the lemmaID '>aHojam_1' as is the stem *ÂHjm* (past/perfect)) of the verb "to abstain, recoil, withdraw". In this way, all morphological variants of a word belong to one cluster.

Table 2. Clustering example

Word	Stems	Example Clusters:
Hjmy	*Hjmy, Hjm*	**Hjm**: Hjmy Hjm ÂHjm
ÂHjm	*ÂHjm, Hjm*	**tnĎyr**: tnĎyry tnĎyr
qAsmy	*qAsmy, qAsm*	**smς**: smςy smςAn Âsmς tsmς smς
tqAsm	*tqAsm, qAsm*	**fDAŷ**: fDAŷy fDAŷ wDAŷ DAŷn
		byr: byr kbyr byrty lbyryA lbyry byry byrA
		dbr: tdbr Âdbr dbry dbr
		qAsm: tqAsm qAsm qAsmy

This technique showed a further 10% increase in coverage of four-word or longer phrases. Nearly 40% of unseen text could be matched to n-grams with $n \geq 4$ in our generalized corpus; approximately 80% of unseen text was covered by 3-grams or better. Compared to the 50% 3-gram matches and 17% 4-gram matches we saw in our original UTF-8 text with no generalization, these were substantial improvements. The results from each of the methods are displayed in Figure 1. Improvements were obtained for all n-grams considered, but we were especially noteworthy for the longer 3 and 4-gram matches, which contain more context and lead to more accurate translations. Clusters were learned from the corpus at training time; at runtime, the input to be translated was analyzed in the same way but could not modify the learned clusters.

	2-gram matches	3-gram matches	4-gram matches
UTF8	0.842	0.565	0.190
Stemmed	0.914	0.638	0.259
LemmaID	0.922	0.664	0.281
Clustering	0.950	0.755	0.393

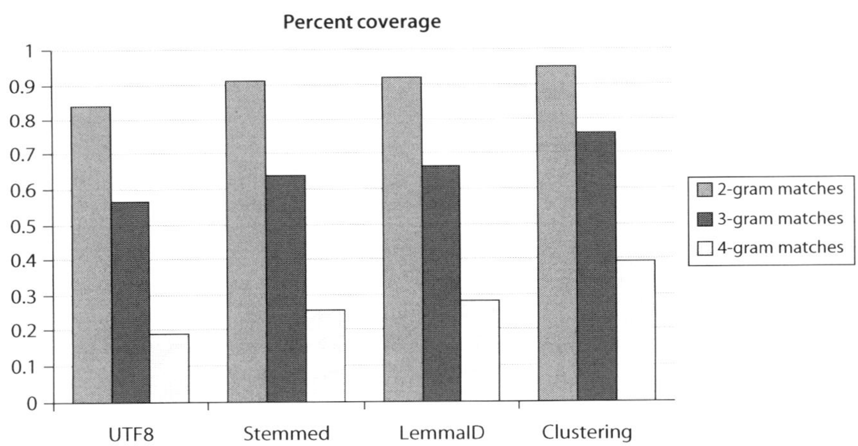

Figure 1. n-gram coverage for different generalization methods

3.2.2 *Filtering*

Having generalized to improve coverage of unseen text, we then had to reduce the ambiguity introduced through over-generalization. We postulated that, if we generalized by stemming the words, we could select the closest match by comparing the morphological features of the input text with the morphological features of each example in our corpus. Unfortunately, the multiple analyses produced by BAMA undermine this approach, because we do not know which features are correct when the word is analyzed out-of-context. We also tried merging all the possible morphological features and see what percentage of them matched, but neither of these context-insensitive approaches worked very well.

What did work well was to save the original surface form of the word along with all possible stems of this surface form. If two words share the same surface form, then we have a near exact translation and we prefer these matches over generalized ones, guaranteeing that we will have all the same matches that would occur if the text did not undergo any generalization. However, if no surface form matches exist, then we select the example(s) in the corpus that share a possible stem with the text we are attempting to translate. Recall that stems are clustered into groups that have some possible analysis in common. Each cluster contains many possible stems, but not all stems present in a cluster are valid analyses of all surface forms that are associated with the cluster. We know that every possible stem of a word will be in the same cluster, but that does not mean that two different words in the same cluster will have the same analysis. Likely, the two words will only have one or two stems in common. By comparing the possible stems of the words in the input and the examples retrieved from the corpus,we effectively reduce the large clusters we built to smaller classes that represent words that are truly ambiguous and could have the same stem as the word we are looking to translate.

An example will clarify the above description. Consider the sentence "5 ملايين طن قمح روسي لمصر" ("5 *mlAyyn Tn qmH rwsy lmSr*") "5 million tons of Russian wheat to Egypt". First, each word in the sentence is matched to a cluster; some clusters contain many words and some only contain a single word. The clusters for this sentence are shown in Table 3.

Table 3. Clusters and metadata associated with the sentence "5 ملايين طن قمح روسي لمصر" ("5 *mlAyyn Tn qmH rwsy lmSr*") "5 million tons of Russian wheat to Egypt"

Word	Cluster	Metadata
mlAyyn	mlAyyn	(SURFACE mlAyyn) (ALT_STEM malAyiyn)
Tn	wT	(SURFACE Tn) (ALT_STEM Tan~) (ALT_STEM Tun~)
qmH	qmH	(SURFACE qmH) (ALT_STEM qamoH) (ALT_STEM qam~aH)
rwsy	rws	(SURFACE rwsy) (ALT_STEM ruws) (ALT_STEM ruwsiy~)
lmSr	mSr	(SURFACE lmSr) (ALT_STEM muSir~) (ALT_STEM miSor)

When training the EBMT engine on this text, the cluster is used by the EBMT engine to index each word. We also store metadata consisting of the original surface form of the word and all possible alternate stems in the EBMT index. When we attempt to translate this sentence we do the reverse process. First, for each word, we look up all examples that share the same cluster. Then we determine if any of the examples have the same surface form, which is the most precise match we can make. Failing any surface form matches, we check to see if any of the examples have an alternate stem in common. This filtering process allows us to match only the closest example(s) from our training corpus. Note that, though one cluster will match many stems, finding a sequence of three or more clusters is strong evidence, coming from local context, that you have found an example similar to the input.

3.2.3 *Generalization and filtering are not enough*

The two charts in Figure 2, on the next page, show the difference between EBMT with generalization and without, describing the EBMT output for the sentence "عزة ابراهسم يستقبل مسؤولا اقتصاديا سعوديا" ("*Ezħ AbrAhym ystqbl msŵwlA AqtSAdyA sςwdyA*") "Izzat Ibrahim meets a Saudi economic official". The top chart (with the Arabic characters) depicts our original system. The bottom chart depicts what happens when we use the methods described above for generalization and filtering. The input sentence in the bottom chart looks different from the input because each word has been replaced with a cluster. Aside from the proper name "Izzat Ibrahim", all entries in the top chart are single word translations.[5] The bottom chart shows that we are now able to retrieve the bigram "economic official". This is important because the word-for-word translation would not get the proper ordering of 'economic' and 'official'. The bottom chart also shows variants of the single word translations ('economic' and 'economy'; 'officials' and 'official') which are a direct result of the morphological generalization. Here they are unnecessary, because we already have a bigram covering that span of text, but often they are helpful. Lastly, as a result of increasing coverage, extraneous translations may appear in the chart. "Official will" is in the generalized chart, but is not an appropriate translation. It is likely the result of 'official' properly generalizing, but also having a poor alignment such that [ya]sotaqobil (يستقبل) "he receives" is aligned to 'will' alone, instead of "will receive", which would be a reasonable translation for the Arabic verb. Recall that stems are being used, hence the prefix ي (ya) is not in the chart. It should be noted that while we want to limit spurious translations, it is normal to have some due in part to generalization and in part to imperfect alignment. In some cases the spurious translations include words that seem to come out of nowhere and are aptly named 'hallucinations'.

Generalization through clustering increased the number of matches in the corpus. Combined with filtering, it avoided overgeneralization in the candidate translations posted by the EBMT component for the language modeler (LM) to compose and choose. However, though we could see substantial improvement in the translation candidates obtained, no actual improvement in translation quality occurred. The LM, being sensitive to *n*-gram occurrences in actual target text on

5. The actual name of the official referred to here is probably Azza Ibrahim, but it was transliterated variously as Izzat and Ezzat in the corpus, as shown in Figure 2 below.

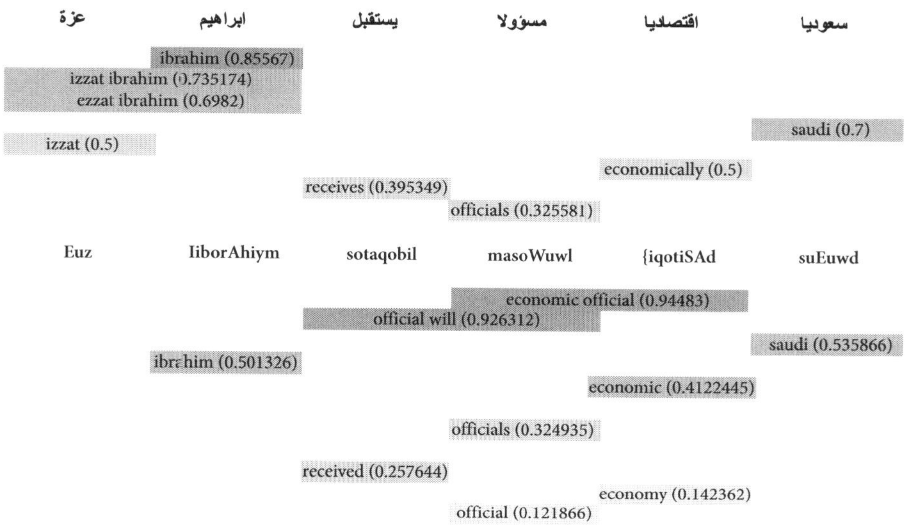

Figure 2. Charts for "عزة ابراهيم يستقبل مسؤولا اقتصاديا سعوديا" ("*Ezħ AbrAhym ystqbl msŵwlA AqtSAdyA sςwdyA*") "Izzat Ibrahim meets a Saudi economic official"

which it was trained, would not select fragment translations that had the right meaning but morphological features that were incorrect for the context due to generalization. The next task was then to focus on improving the interaction between the translations generated after generalization and the LM, while continuing to investigate to what extent the filtering process could be further refined by using additional morphological information.

3.3 Phase 2: Generalization, filtering and adaptation

In the second phase of our work, we focused on enriching the generalization and filtering techniques and using information in the source sentence to adapt translation candidates. The resulting system demonstrates a performance that scales well with the size of training data and provides additional improvement even with large corpora.

3.3.1 *Generalization*

The morphological generalization technique we adopted in this phase is an extension of the clustering technique described previously: clustering is done over lemmaIDs instead of stems. Though generalizing a word with its lemmaID does reduce the ambiguity, often a single word can still be analyzed as having several different meanings (and thus different lemmaIDs). Therefore, we need to abstract above the level of a single lemmaID by forming clusters that represent several lemmaIDs. We assign each lemmaID to be a member of one cluster. The goal is to have all lemmaIDs that can be derived from an Arabic word exist in the same cluster and tag each Arabic word with a token representing that cluster. Because the cluster represents several lemmaIDs, it maintains the ambiguity of the analyses. Every possible analysis of the Arabic word results in a lemmaID that is present in that cluster. However, this does not mean that every lemmaID present in the cluster is a valid analysis of the Arabic word. The clusters are not unique to each word; rather, they are shared by many words. Thus, there may well be extra lemmaIDs present in a cluster, which will be filtered out at run time.

Theoretically, the number of lemmaIDs contained within each cluster is unimportant. In practice, very large clusters are quite inefficient because the number of lemmaIDs in each cluster is proportional to how many examples we must look for in our corpus at run time. The degree of morphological ambiguity in Arabic renders the goal of having all lemmaIDs derivable from a word in the same cluster infeasible because some clusters are simply too large.[6] So we relax this restriction and form clusters of lemmaIDs such that most analyses of a word result in lemmaIDs that occur together in one cluster. At runtime the system is limited to looking up matches using the lemmaIDs contained in one cluster. If two lemmaIDs are possible analyses of an Arabic word and they are not in the same cluster, then matches are sought using one lemmaID only. Performance would be no worse than if no generalization was present, but the system will not perform at its full potential.

In order to build the clusters described above, we rephrase the problem as a graph clustering problem. Graph clustering supports building clusters from strongly connected words and clusters can be split if they get too large. First we plot all the lemmaIDs on a graph. Then we analyze every word that could be generated using combinations of stems and affixes from the BAMA lexicon. For each word we build a fully connected graph of the set of lemmaIDs that were possible analyses of the word. If a connection between two lemmaIDs already exists, we increment the weight of the connection. As an example, consider the analyses of the surface form وكتابي *wktAby* given in Table 4. Once the prefix 'و' '*w*' (and) is stripped off, there are still alternative stems with different suffixes and different case markings (some written, some not). Figure 3 below shows how a cluster could be built from BAMA using the lemmaIDs and stems.

6. In particular, one cluster contained over 2,000 lemmaIDs and occurred frequently.

Table 4. All morphological analyses of وكتابي *wktAby*

lemmaID	Morphological analysis							
kitAbiy~_1	*wa* 'and'	+	*kitAbiy~* 'writing/ written'					
kitAbiy~_1	*wa* 'and'	+	*kitAbiy~* 'writing/ written'	+	*u* [def.nom.]			
kitAbiy~_1	*wa* 'and'	+	*kitAbiy~* 'writing/ written'	+	*a* [def.acc.]			
kitAbiy~_1	*wa* 'and'	+	*kitAbiy~* 'writing/ written'	+	*i* [def.gen.]			
kitAbiy~_1	*wa* 'and'	+	*kitAbiy~* 'writing/ written'	+	*N* [indef.nom.]			
kitAbiy~_1	*wa* 'and'	+	*kitAbiy~* 'writing/ written'	+	*K* [indef.gen.]			
kitAb_1	*wa* 'and'	+	*kitAb* 'book'	+	*ayo* 'two' [acc.]			
kitAb_1	*wa* 'and'	+	*kitAb* 'book'	+	*ayo* 'two' [acc.]	+	*ya* 'my'	
kitAb_1	*wa* 'and'	+	*kitAb* 'book'	+	*ayo* 'two' [gen.]			
kitAb_1	*wa* 'and'	+	*kitAb* 'book'	+	*ayo* 'two' [gen.]	+	*ya* 'my'	
kitAb_1	*wa* 'and'	+	*kitAb* 'book'	+	*iy* 'my'			
kut~Ab_1	*wa* 'and'	+	*kut~Ab* 'village school'	+	*iy* 'my'			
kAtib_1	*wa* 'and'	+	*kut~Ab* 'authors/ writers'	+	*iy* 'my'			

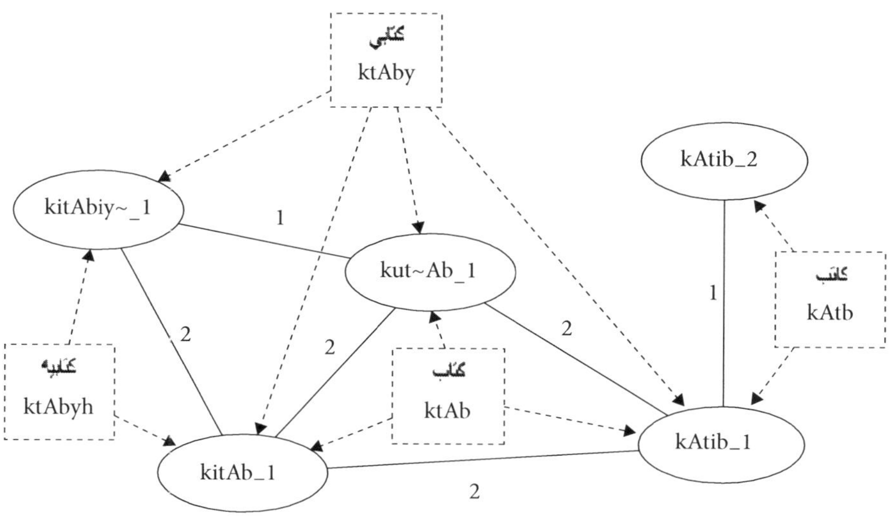

Figure 3. Example of clustering. Each ellipse is a lemmaID. Dotted boxes and lines are not part of the graph but are provided to illustrate the Arabic words that result in this graph structure

To further ensure accuracy, we also adjust the weighted graph by the unigram probability of each lemmaID as calculated from the LDC Arabic Treebank (Maamouri et al. 2004). Clustering is done using a technique developed by (van Dongen 2000) and the freely available MCL toolkit.[7] The algorithm randomly walks through the graph to determine areas of high connectivity. Parameters given to MCL allow us to adjust the required amount of interconnectivity and thus the size of the clusters.

The clusters so formed are used to transform the text so that we can look up all morphological forms of a word with one token. Each word in the text is replaced by a token – the name of the cluster to which it belonged. In addition, we annotate the text with information about the original form of the word and its possible morphological features from BAMA; the information is used later to identify the best translations. We perform this process on both training text and evaluation text.[8]

3.3.2 *Filtering and adaptation*

At runtime the EBMT engine looks for examples that will yield the correct English translation, searching for Arabic matches based on the clustering described above. When an example is retrieved, it is only a possible match, since clusters are often broad and overgeneralize. Two more steps are needed: (1) determining which examples in the training data are true morphological generalizations and which are noise created by the clustering; (2) optionally adapting the translation of some of the examples in the corpus if the morphological features differ.

We iterate through each possible morphological analysis of the text to be translated and all matches from the corpus to determine the similarity of each pair of analyses. If the surface forms are equal, it is a perfect match; otherwise, we determine if we have a valid generalization by comparing lemmaIDs. We discard an example if any word in it does not share a possible lemmaID with the corresponding word in the input text. For remaining examples we compare morphological features.

To be a valid translation candidate, some morphological features such as part of speech and person must be the same. It is necessary that these features do not change in order to recover a proper English translation. This is a stricter constraint than the one that was placed on matching in Phase 1 of the work, but a necessary one for doing adaptation on the target side. Features such as gender and case are allowed to be different because, most of the time, these features have the same realization in English. Even if the realization is occasionally different, it results in an acceptable translation and the LM will select the most likely combination of

7. Available at http://micans.org/mcl/.

8. As the process is external to the EBMT system, a different morphological analyzer could be used, so the technique could be easily applied to a different language.

phrases in the end. It is usually better to get a long match with slightly incorrect morphological features than a word by word translation or short matches.

Additionally, we allow matches with morphological features that alter the English translation, if the change is easily defined. Here, the system dynamically modifies the English translation via a rewrite rule to match the morphological change. For example, one of the most common adjustments made is to account for the prolific use of initial وَ *wa* in Arabic. The prefix *wa* is identified by BAMA as a conjunction clitic, and our system marks the phrase with the morphological feature CONJ. Sometimes *wa* is translated as 'and', but frequently it is dropped from the English translation. In its unvoweled form, *wa* appears simply as *w*. Although we may not have seen the phrase والكتاب القديم *wAlktAb Alqdym* we may have seen الكتاب القديم *AlktAb Alqdym* translated as "the old book". In this case we do not know if the 'and', due to the presence of *w*, should actually appear in the English translation. Thus we put both "the old book" and "and the old book" into the lattice and rely on the LM to select the correct phrase in context. Similarly, the system will add or remove words from the English translation to account for the presence or absence of prepositions and definite markers in the Arabic text.

Allowing generalization to occur over morphological features that alter the English translation, and then recovering a valid English translation through rewrite rules, significantly enhanced coverage. While there a few morphological features that do not usually change the translation, they occur infrequently. Instead, it is very common to find two translations that are subtly different (for example, one uses a different preposition or is marked as definite and the other does/is not). These changes can easily be captured and adjusted for with rewrite rules, allowing our system to increase coverage and generate examples that do not exist in the corpus.

Table 5. Types of morphological generalizations

Not allowed	Allowed without modifications	Allowed with modifications
– Part of Speech	– Gender (not nouns)	– Definiteness
– Aspect	– Case (accusative and nominative only)	– Negativity
– Voice	– Mood	– Possessive Pronouns
		– Nominative Pronouns
		– Conjunctions
		– Prepositions
		– *Person*
		– *Number*
		– *Acc. Pronouns*

Table 5 shows the features over which the system could generalize. There are still some features (in *italics*) that are slightly more complex for which we did not code the rewrite rules. Number, for example, is simple in the singular and plural, but Arabic has a dual number that might appear as a plural or some permutation of 'both' or "two of" in the English text.

3.3.3 *Scoring*

For each example, the EBMT engine returns a heuristic score that roughly represents its alignment quality. This score is then modified by a weight that reflects how much generalization was required for the example to match, considering morphological similarity and using a strong preference for sharing the same stems. A perfect match obviously receives more weight than a heavily generalized match. The scores for all examples that resulted in the same target text fragment are summed together and divided by the total of all examples to produce a probability for each translation.

Proper scoring of generalizations is critical. Initially, each morphological feature had a predefined weight and the scoring was multiplicative. A morphological generalization that had a change in definiteness and gender would be the product of the weights for definiteness and gender, but the system's performance was suboptimal.

We ran the system on parts of the 2003 NIST MT Evaluation (MT03) data and compared the generalized matches to four reference translations. An example was marked as correct if its translation was found among the reference translations and incorrect otherwise. Short matches (those containing a single word or whose total length was less than 10 characters) were excluded. When we ran tests to see how often each generalization was correct, the results were surprising. Table 6 partially summarizes the generalizations performed on trigram examples retrieved from the corpus. The percentage next to each line indicates how often the generalization was correct. Each set of parenthesis indicates the morphological generalizations (if any) performed at that position in the phrase.

The table illustrates that removing a preposition in the first word of a trigram is much more likely to be correct than removing a preposition later in the phrase. Thus, we needed to score differently based on the location of the generalization. Furthermore, the score for a combined value does not appear to be related to its individual scores. Inserting or removing a definite article at the beginning of a trigram has approximately the same probability. However, inserting a definite article and removing a preposition at the beginning of a trigram is much more likely to result in a correct translation than removing a definite article and removing a preposition at the same location. This demonstrates that the scoring must be based off training data and have different probabilities for each possible combination of morphological features. The probabilities will not be exact, and by the nature of our tests looking for exact string matches, they are likely to be somewhat sparse. However, the final score for a translation usually depends on many different generalizations, so an inexact weight for one generalization will not greatly affect the overall scores.

Table 6. Frequency of correctness of some morphological generalizations

11%	() () (Preposition Removal)
13%	() (Preposition Removal) ()
81%	(Preposition Removal) () ()
34%	(Definite Insertion) () ()
31%	(Definite Removal) () ()
48%	(Preposition Removal + Definite Insertion) () ()
23%	(Preposition Removal + Definite Removal) () ()

The final score for each translation is an interpolation of its score for each type of generalization. The interpolation weights are what we determine from training data, with non-generalized examples given a weight of 1.0. Conceptually, we can think of the system as having different corpora for each type of generalization and combining together the examples it finds from each corpora.

3.3.4 *Results*

We evaluated our approach by building one system with a large training corpus – 1.4 million sentences pairs including newswire text and sections of the UN Arabic-English Parallel Text (LDC2004E13) – and another one with a small training corpus – 50,000 sentence pairs.[9] We expected the morphological processing to bring large gains when data was scarce, but we wanted to see if our system could still improve performance when very large amounts of training data were available.

9. Newswire includes AFA, AFP, ANN, ASB, eTIRR, Ummah 2006, and Xinhua.

Each system was evaluated on the 2004 and 2005 NIST MT Evaluation data sets (MT04 and MT05). Each of these datasets contains four human reference translations. MT04 contains editorial, speech, and news genres, but nearly half of it is news. We wanted to perform multiple evaluations to determine when morphological generalization is beneficial, but also maintain enough sentences to have meaningful results. We split MT04 by genre, and divided the news into two parts – one from Xinhua News Agency and the other from Agence France Press. MT05 contains only news text from Xinhua News Agency and Agence France Press; we split it into four chunks from each source, approximately the same size as the MT04 chunks. Document boundaries were preserved in all the splits and the chunks ranged in size from 251 sentences to 387 sentences.

The MT03 dataset was used to tune parameters controlling the number of translation candidates, length ratio, reorder penalty, language model weighting, and the like. The tuning process evaluated 26 random starting points and then maximized the best starting point through hill-climbing. To avoid inadvertently finding a local maximum, the procedure was done twice on each data set. The parameters were tuned for the baseline system which does not include the morphological generalizations. Weights for the morphological generalizations were determined separately also using the MT03 dataset. However, the system that included the morphological generalizations used the same tuned system parameters from the baseline.

Figure 4, on the next page, shows the results of the evaluation. Using morphological generalization produces a noticeable and statistically significant improvement over the baseline for both small and large dataset. The data also confirms our expectations that improvement for the small system is higher than the large system. With a lot of data the corpus contains more exact matches of the phrases we are trying to translate; therefore morphological generalization is not needed as frequently. Nonetheless, the use of generalization still improves the baseline 3 to 11%. It supports our conjecture that, due to the complexity of Arabic morphology, there can be many phrases we have not seen before even with a large corpus. Moreover, we observe that our approach seemed to help the speech genre more than other genres, but with substantial variation therein. The news genre also showed fluctuating improvements across different test sets (likely due to the different news sources and document topics) but generalization improved the mean and decreased the variance in this genre. Most significantly, the use of generalization never resulted in a lower score than the baseline, so the approach seems appropriate across different genres and data set sizes.

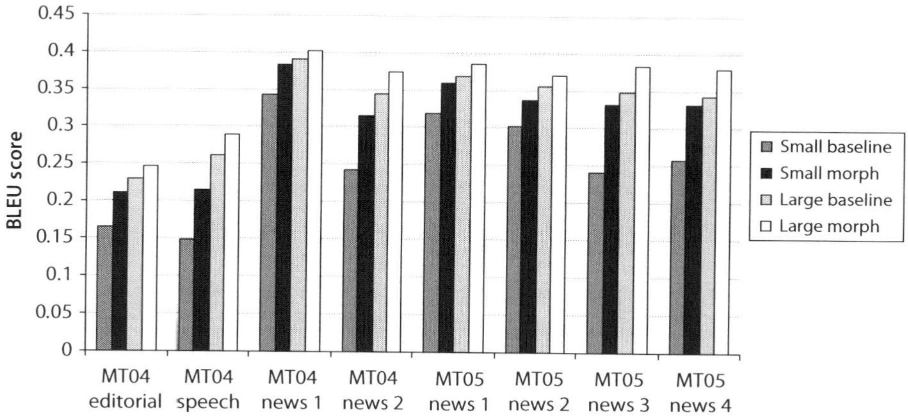

	MT04 editorial	MT04 speech	MT04 news 1	MT04 news 2	MT05 news 1	MT05 news 2	MT05 news 3	MT05 news 4
Small baseline	0.1640	0.1480	0.3431	0.2429	0.3191	0.3014	0.2409	0.2574
Small morph	0.2114	0.2153	0.3841	0.3153	0.3585	0.3363	0.3315	0.3306
Small Improv.	28.90%	45.47%	11.95%	29.81%	12.35%	11.58%	37.61%	28.44%
Large baseline	0.2293	0.2604	0.3911	0.3436	0.3680	0.3550	0.3482	0.3434
Large morph	0.2466	0.2897	0.4027	0.3741	0.3856	0.3696	0.3836	0.3803
Large improv.	7.54%	11.25%	2.97%	8.88%	4.78%	4.11%	10.17%	10.75%

Figure 4. System performance in BLEU with and without morphological generalization

4. Related work

Before summarizing and concluding, we briefly review how other EBMT and SMT systems have incorporated morphology, especially in translating from morphologically complex languages. A comparison with other EBMT systems is hard because the Pangloss-Lite framework we use (Frederking & Brown 1996) is quite different. Pangloss-lite is a Multi-Engine MT system: different translation engines propose partial or full translations placing their output on a lattice with a score of the estimated value of each candidate. The LM component selects and composes candidates using multiple criteria. We worked within this framework, using just the EBMT engine to select multi-word fragment translations and a statistical dictionary for single word translations and alignment.

The closest reference point for our work is the generalization capabilities already built into the EBMT engine we are using. There are two related mechanisms. The first establishes classes of words or phrases in the source language – and corresponding translation in the target language – that are syntactically interchangeable (some restrictions apply). The second allows adding morphological and syntactic information directly in the corpus as general ways to map between source and target language structures. Both mechanisms generalize the corpus by abstracting away from specific words. They have been shown to substantially increase the work performed by a parallel corpus of a limited size (or, equivalently, reduce the amount of text required to achieve the same performance) for Spanish-English and French-English translation, but require hand-coding of the classes and rules and a tagged corpus (Brown 1999). Later work (Brown 2000) used monolingual word clustering techniques to perform bilingual word clustering on French-English documents and achieved much the same results with no manual intervention, especially when clusters were seeded with a little information.

Carl (1999) induced German-English translation templates from examples. Source-side morphological information was represented as feature bundles and a shallow syntactic rule formalism was used to percolate features into derivation trees, but no features were transferred from the source to the target language. All features necessary to generate the appropriate target language strings were contained in the target language feature bundles which were retrieved from the example-base. McTait (2001) maintained ambiguous analyses on the source side and generated possible combinations on the target side, pruning them by applying morphological constraints. But he worked in English-to-French translation and therefore with limited source-side morphological variation.

More recent work in Bengali-English translation (Anwarus Salam et al. 2009) handles morphology using a strategy of 'morpho' word and suffix replacement, addition and deletion. Bar & Dershowitz (2011) use EBMT on Arabic-English translation. They apply different levels of matching, including morphological level matching in context (text, stem, lemma, and part-of-speech), assigning to exact text strings and stem matches the maximum score, while lemma and part-of-speech level matches receive less credit in the combined score for the fragment. In their contribution to the present book (following chapter), they present an approach to generalizing matching based on words that are semantic equivalents in context. As in our work, the impact of their treatment is more clearly seen with a small number of examples, where the use of contextual synonyms enable the EBMT to better exploit the available data.

While our approach to morphological generalization differs substantially from approaches adopted by other EBMT systems, past and present, there were several relevant attempts to use morphology in SMT prior to and concurrently with our work. (Nießen & Ney 2000; Lee 2004; Sadat & Habash 2006; Zollmann et al. 2006) all present techniques that select a morphological analysis and split the source text in a manner that closely reflects the English translation. The last three specifically address techniques for Arabic. (Sadat & Habash 2006) study the effect of different morphological preprocessing decisions and the size of the training data. They conclude that an English-like segmentation scheme works well for Arabic on small data sets, but for large datasets splitting only conjunction clitics and particles performs better. That line of research was further elaborated and is described in Chapter 5 of this book.

Conceptually, the most similar work to ours is that of (Nießen & Ney 2004) and (Yang & Kirchhoff 2006). (Nießen & Ney 2004) describe an SMT system that uses a generalized hierarchical lexicon with morphological features for German-English translation. (Yang & Kirchhoff 2006) describe a statistical system that generalizes over the phrase table through a back-off model with examples in German-English and Finnish-English translation; however, their work only uses stemming and compound splitting and no other generalization over individual words. Though our approach bears conceptual similarity to both of these, the difference in languages and corpora used makes any direct comparison of results not meaningful.

5. Summary and conclusions

We have described an approach that improves the output quality of Arabic-to-English Example-Based MT by generalizing over morphological features. Our approach takes into consideration two challenges: the need to generalize when faced with data sparseness and the excessive ambiguity that it may result in. Data sparseness occurs with low resource languages due to limited corpora, but the problem is also connected with morphologically complex languages. For the latter, the potential for multiple surface realizations of words makes it less likely that a data-driven translation method will find exact matches to guide translation of a given input. Both input and corpus text must be generalized to find one or more inexact matches. Unfortunately, in so doing, overgeneralization may occur, especially in Arabic, where the written form can be highly ambiguous due to orthographic practices. Therefore generalization must be combined with a way of maintaining and using the original form of the word, in addition to its multiple analyses and associated features, to find more and better matches and to adapt the best one(s), if needed and if possible, to the new context of use.

Our approach relies on the strength of EBMT and performs fuzzy matching of morphological features across entire phrases. Using morphologically similar phrases is especially helpful in language pairs such as Arabic-English where word order is different at a phrasal level. We address the issue of data sparseness by generalizing over text that the system has seen and, in this way, find more examples of translation of unseen text. Instead of building a corpus that uses the final form of Arabic words, we enhance coverage by using a more general representation of each word. We experimented with different ways of generalizing and found that creating clusters of related lemmaIDs was a useful approach, as long as the clusters do not get too large.

To avoid unnecessary and potentially dangerous generalizations, we also keep track of information from the original surface form of each word and pass it along at runtime as 'metadata' to select the best possible translation. When the morphological features of the input and the best matched example differ, the system automatically attempts to alter the English translation through rewrite rules. The scoring of translation candidates is sensitive to the types of generalizations performed and therefore must be determined from training data. The appropriateness of a single generalization depends on where in an *n*-gram it occurs (Table 6 above) and the scores of multiple simultaneous generalizations are not a simple function of the scores of individual ones. So we must estimate different scores for each possible combination of morphological features.

The resulting system is able to effectively translate Arabic phrases it has never seen before based on morphologically similar phrases. It can do so because it is able to find more matches, select and score them based on the type of generalization required, and adapt them so that the LM has a better chance of choosing them. This processing, in effect, extends the coverage of the training corpus, which also increases accuracy of translation. Its impact was demonstrated by an evaluation using both a small and a large training corpus and on different genres of text. While, as expected, our approach produced greater improvements over the baseline with the small training corpus, there were also noteworthy increases over the baseline for large training corpora. Overall, the processing strikingly boosted results for test sets that had underperformed with the baseline system (news, editorial and, most of all, speech). It also never resulted in a lower score than the baseline no matter what the size of the training set.

Our approach lies somewhere between traditional EBMT and SMT systems in terms of its goals and the techniques used. Like EBMT, it performs better than SMT on smaller corpora, using generalization to make the corpus go further, but it improves BLEU scores even when trained on corpus sizes typical of SMT.

Our approach is more effective than those used by its contemporaries because morphemes are not split off, which allows matching morphological changes anywhere in a phrase. It also handles morphological ambiguity and includes rewrite rules to allow for a wider range of generalization. Moreover, the rewrite rules are the only Arabic-specific component of the system, so minimal work would be required to apply our approach to another language.

References

Anwarus Salam, K. M. D., M. Khan, and T. Nishino. 2009. Example Based English-Bengali machine translation using WordNet. In *Triangle Symposium on Advanced ICT.* Tokyo.

Bar, K., and N. Dershowitz. 2011. Using verb paraphrases for Arabic-to-English example-base translation. In *Machine Translation and Morphologically-rich Languages: Research Workshop of the Israel Science Foundation*, University of Haifa, Israel, 23 January.

Brown, P. F., J. Cocke, S. A. Della Pietra, V. J. Della Pietra, F. Jelinek, J. D. Lafferty, R. Mercer, and P. S. Roosin. 1990. A statistical approach to machine translation. *Computational Linguistics* 16(1): 79–85.

Brown, R. D. 1996. Example-based machine translation in the Pangloss System. In *Proceedings of the 16th International Conference on Computational Linguistics* (COLING-96), Copenhagen, Denmark, August 5–9, 169–174.

Brown, R. D. 1999. Adding linguistic knowledge to a lexical example-based translation system. In *Proceedings of the Eighth International Conference on Theoretical and Methodological Issues in Machine* Translation (TMI-99), Chester, UK, August, 22–32.

Brown, R. D. 2000. Automated generalization of Translation examples. In *Proceedings of the Eighteenth International Conference on Computational Linguistics* (COLING-2000), Saarbrücken, Germany, August, 125–131.

Buckwalter, T. 2004. *Buckwalter Arabic Morphological Analyzer Version 2.0.* LDC2004L02

Callison-Burch, C. 2007. Paraphrasing and Translation. Ph.D. dissertation, University of Edinburgh.

Carl, M. 1999. Inducing translation templates for example-based machine translation. *MT Summit VII*, Singapore, 617–624.

Carl, M., and A. Way. 2003. *Recent Advances in Example-Based Machine Translation.* Dordrecht: Kluwer.

Frederking, R. E., and R. D. Brown. 1996. The Pangloss-lite machine translation system. In *Expanding MT Horizons: Proceedings of the Second Conference of the Association for Machine Translation in the Americas* (AMTA-96), Montreal, Canada, 268–272.

Habash, N., and O. Rambow. 2005. Arabic tokenization, morphological analysis, and part-of-speech tagging in one fell swoop. In *Proceedings of the Conference of American Association for Computational Linguistics* (ACL'05).

Lee, Y.-S. 2004. Morphological analysis for statistical machine translation. In *Proceedings of the Human Language Technology and North American Association for Computational Linguistics Conference.*

McTait, K. 2001. Memory-based translation using translation patterns. In *Proceedings of the 4th Annual CLUK Colloquium*, 43–52, Sheffield, UK, 2001.

Maamouri, M., A. Bies, T. Buckwalter, and W. Mekki. 2004. The Penn Arabic Treebank: Building a large-scale annotated Arabic corpus. In *NEMLAR International Conference on Arabic Language Resources and Tools*, 102–109, 2004

Nagao, M. 1984. A framework of mechanical translation between Japanese and English by analogy principle. In *Artificial and Human Intelligence*. Alick Elithorn & Rana Banerji (eds), 173–180. North-Holland.

Nießen, S., and H. Ney. 2000. Improving SMT quality with morpho-syntactic analysis. In *The 18th International Conference on Computational Linguistics*.

Nießen, S., and H. Ney. 2004. Statistical machine translation with scarce resources using morpho-syntactic information. *Computational Linguistics* 30(2): 181–204.

Phillips, A. B., and V. Cavalli-Sforza. 2006. Arabic-to-English example based machine translation using context-insensitive morphological analysis. In *Proceedings of Journée d'Etudes sur le Traitement Automatique de la Langue Arabe*. Institut d'Etudes et de Recherches pour l'Arabisation, June 5–6, Rabat, Morocco.

Phillips, A. B., V. Cavalli-Sforza, and R. D. Brown. 2007. Improving example based machine translation through morphological generalization and adaptation. In *Machine Translation Summit XI*, Copenhagen, Denmark, September 10–14.

Roukos, S., D. Graff, and D. Melamed. 1995. *Hansard French/English*. Philadelphia PA: Linguistic Data Consortium.

Sadat, F., and N. Habash. 2006. Arabic preprocessing schemes for statistical machine translation. In *Proceedings of Human Language Technology Conference of the NAACL*.

Somers, H. 2003. An overview of EBMT. In *Recent Advances in Example-Based Machine Translation*, Michael Carl & Andy Way (eds), 3–57. Dordrecht: Kluwer.

van Dongen, S. 2000. Graph Clustering by Flow Simulation. Ph.D. dissertation, University of Utrecht.

Yang, M., and K. Kirchoff. 2006. Phrase-based backoff models for machine translation of highly inflected languages. In *Proceedings of the European Chapter of the ACL*.

Zimmer, B. 2010. On language chunking. *The New York Times Magazine*. September 16, 2010.

Zollmann, A., A.Venugopal, and S. Vogel. 2006. Bridging the inflection morphology gap for Arabic statistical machine translation. In *Proceedings of the Human Language Technology Conference of the NAACL*, Companion Volume: Short Papers, 201–204.

Using semantic equivalents for Arabic-to-English example-based translation

Kfir Bar* & Nachum Dershowitz
School of Computer Science, Tel Aviv University, Ramat Aviv, Israel

We explore the effect of using Arabic semantic equivalents in an example-based Arabic-English translation system. We describe two experiments using single-word equivalents in translation as test cases for broadening the level of similarity and using multi-word Arabic paraphrases in the future. In the first experiment, we used synonymous Arabic nouns, derived from a lexicon, to help locate potential translation examples for fragments of a given input sentence. Not surprisingly, the smaller the parallel corpus, the greater the contribution provided by synonyms. Considering the degree of relevance of the subject matter of a potential match contributes to the quality of the final results. In the second experiment, we used automatically extracted single-word verb paraphrases, derived from a corpus of comparable documents. The experiments were performed within an implementation of a non-structural example-based translation system, using a parallel corpus aligned at the sentence level. The methods developed here should apply to other morphologically-rich languages.

1. Introduction

Corpus-based translation systems use existing parallel texts to guide the translation process. One of the main problems, when using a corpus-based system for translation, is the relatively small quantity of data that the system may have available for the purpose. Callison-Burch, in his thesis (Callison-Burch 2007), measured the effect of the size of the parallel-corpus used in a statistical Spanish-to-English translation system on the amount of covered n-grams in the resultant translations. His results show a clear increase in coverage as the corpus grows larger, but even when the corpus contains relatively many words, many three- and four-word

* This work was carried out in partial fulfillment of the requirements for a Ph.D. degree at Tel Aviv University.

sequences remain uncovered. We repeated his experiment, but using an example-based Arabic-to-English translation system instead. The results, which are displayed in Figure 1, are more or less similar to those obtained for Spanish. The horizontal axis represents the number of Arabic words in the parallel-corpus used by the system and the vertical axis is the number of translated test-set unique n-grams.

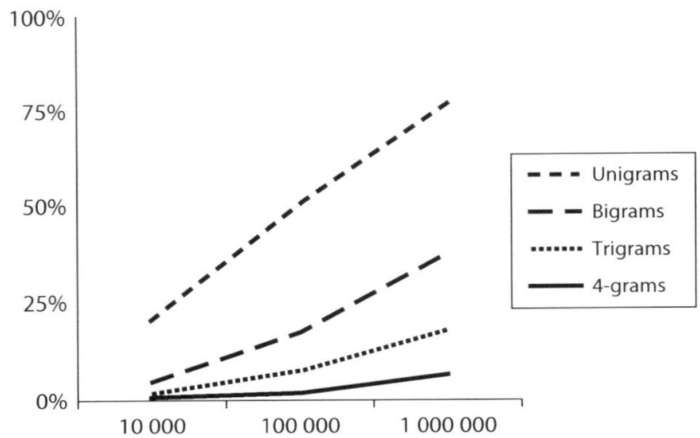

Figure 1. Translation coverage of unique phrases from a test set

One can see that even when the system uses a corpus containing a million tokens, the total number of untranslated n-grams remains high. When translating from a highly inflected language, finding an exact match for an input phrase with reasonable precision presumably requires a very large parallel corpus. Since we are interested in studying the use of relatively small corpora for translation, matching phrases to examples in the corpus should be done on a spectrum of linguistic levels, so that not only exact phrases are discovered, but also related ones. In this chapter, we explore the effect of matching texts based on synonyms and single-word paraphrases.

We describe two experiments in which synonyms were considered in the matching process. In both experiments we used single-word "contextual" synonyms as a case study, with the intention of including longer semantically-replaceable phrases in the future. *Contextual synonyms* are words that are similar in meaning only within particular contexts. Figure 2 shows an example of contextually synonymous verbs in Arabic. The verbs *bv* ("to broadcast") and *nql* ("to convey") are semantic equivalents. One can see that the two sentences are almost the same; they differ only in the verbs. On the right side, the common meaning of the verb *bv*, which is the stem of the word *bvt*, is "to broadcast", and on the left side, the common meaning of the verb *nql* (stem for *nqlt*) is "to convey". However, both sentences need to be translated in the same way – "the radio broadcast these songs". That means that the two verbs are exchangeable in this context (radio broadcasts) and are, therefore, semantic equivalents.

وقد <u>نقلت</u> الاذاعة هذه الاغاني | **وقد <u>بثت</u> الاذاعة هذه الاغاني**

*wqd <u>**nqlt**</u> AlA*AEp h*h AlAgAny* | *wqd <u>**bvt**</u> AlA*AEp h*h AlAgAny*

The radio <u>broadcast</u> these songs

Figure 2. Example of two semantically equivalent words

Hereinafter, whenever we use the word "synonym", we will mean such a contextual synonym. We will consider different techniques for the extraction of noun and verb synonyms, and will report on the results of both experiments.

Noun synonyms were automatically created for the first experiment using the stem list provided by the Buckwalter (version 1.0) morphological analyzer (Buckwalter 2002). The word-pairs were organized in various levels of perceived synonymy. The quality of the system's resultant translations was measured for each of the different levels.

In using synonyms for matching, we also considered the relevance of the subject matter of translation examples to the given input sentence. Topics were determined using a classifier that was first trained on the English Reuters training corpus and then used for classifying the English part of the translation examples in our parallel corpus. With this classification of the samples in hand, we trained an Arabic-language classifier on the Arabic version of the parallel corpus, which was then used to classify new Arabic input documents.

Experiments were conducted on two English-Arabic corpora, one about twice as large as the other. The system was tested on all levels of synonymy and the effect of using the classification feature at each level was examined. The results, reported in (Bar & Dershowitz 2010), show that, in general, the system performs slightly better when using synonyms.

In the second experiment, we automatically created a list of synonymous verbs and then used them to further the translation process. This time we used a corpus of Arabic "comparable" documents for learning synonym pairs. *Comparable documents* are texts dealing with the same event, but which are not necessarily translations of the same source. The basic learning technique we describe here was implemented merely on verbs, as motivation for future work seeking alternative approaches for learning large sets of (multi-word) Arabic paraphrases and using them to extend the coverage of a corpus-based translation system.

For the purposes of this research, we have developed an experimental Arabic-to-English example-based machine translation (EBMT) system, which exploits a bilingual corpus to find examples that match fragments of the input source-language text – Modern Standard Arabic (MSA), in our case – and imitate its translations. Translation examples were extracted from a collection of parallel, sentence-aligned, unvocalized Arabic-English documents, taken from several corpora published by the Linguistic Data Consortium. The system is non-structural: translation examples are stored as textual strings, with some additional inferred linguistic features.

Ever since first proposed by Nagao (1984), the example-based paradigm has been a fairly common technique for natural language processing (NLP), and especially for machine-translation applications. As mentioned in the previous chapter, the main idea behind example-based machine translation (EBMT) is to translate fragments of the source-language input text based on similar known example translations. Such a process presumably emulates the way a human translator operates in some cases. Since it uses real human-translated data, the resultant translations are usually more fluent than ones created artificially using other translation paradigms.

In general, our system performs three main steps in order to translate a given input sentence: matching, transfer and recombination.

In the *matching step*, the system uses various levels of morphological information to broaden the quantity of matched translation examples and to generate new translations based on morphologically similar fragments. A *match-score* is created for every matched fragment, which is based on the individual words' matching levels. We elaborate more on this score in Section 3. In the *transfer step*, those matched phrases are translated using the target-language (English, in our case) version of a sentence-aligned parallel corpus. For each translated fragment, we calculate a *translation-score*, which is the ratio between the number of translated words and the total number of words in the Arabic part of the fragment. The *total-score* of a fragment is the average of the match-score and the translation-score multiplied by the ratio between the number of input tokens covered by the fragment and the total amount of the input sentence tokens. This formula is the result of several adaptations, based on experiments, and resulted in the best performance.

In the *recombination step,* all the translated fragments are pasted together to form a complete target-language text, usually by preferring larger translated fragments, because they use more context. The recombination process is implemented similar to the way the decoding process is implemented within a statistical translation system. The difference is that recombination is based on the total-score of every fragment, which captures the various aspects of relevancy of a given fragment to the final translation.

We decided to work with an example-based system, rather than a statistical one, mainly because it is the more natural platform for using paraphrases during the translation process. Example-based systems store translations as pairs of strings augmented with some morpho-syntactic information. The source-language part of the examples is indexed on several morphological levels to expedite the on-line matching process. Once a fragment is found, the system calculates its translation score, which is based on the matching levels of the individual words and the number of source-language words covered by the extracted translations. However, it is not based on statistics. Paraphrases can be simply indexed with their translations, extracted using their corresponding source-language corpus fragments. On the other hand, in a statistical translation system, one needs to calculate the translation probability of every paraphrase added to the system's phrase-table. Since the new, added paraphrases are not actually found within the loaded parallel-corpus, these probabilities are usually estimated using various techniques.

The following section summarizes some previous related work. Section 3 contains a general description of our example-based system. In Sections 4 and 5, we describe our experiments with noun and verb synonyms, respectively. In both sections, we provide some experimental results using common automatic evaluation metrics. Some conclusions are suggested in the last section.

2. Related work

Nagao (1984) initiated the example-based approach to machine-translation with a structural Japanese-to-English translation system. Other influential works include (Sato & Nagao 1990; Maruyama & Watanabe 1992; Sumita & Iida 1995; Nirenburg et al. 1994; Brown 1999). This is the style of machine translation we are using in this work.

There are several works dealing with morphologically-rich languages such as Arabic. Nevertheless, we could not find any specific one that measures the effect of using synonyms in the matching step. Among relevant works, there is (Stroppa et al. 2006), an example-based Basque-to-English translation system. That system focuses on extracting translation examples using the marker-based approach integrated with phrase-based statistical machine translation to translate new given inputs. As reported, that combined approach showed significant improvements over state-of-the-art phrase-based statistical translation systems.

The work by Lee (2004) is on improving a statistical Arabic-to-English translation system, based on words as well as phrases, by making the parallel corpus syntactically and morphologically symmetric in a preprocessing stage. This is achieved by segmenting each Arabic word into smaller particles (prefix, stem and suffix), and then omitting some of them in order to make the parallel corpus as symmetric as possible. That method seems to increase evaluation metrics when using a small corpus. Similar conclusions were reached by Sadat and Habash (2006) in their work on improving a statistical Arabic-to-English translation system. There, several morphological preprocessing schemes were applied separately on different size corpora.

In some work on Japanese-to-English example-based machine translation (Nakazawa et al. 2006), synonyms were used in the source language for matching translation examples, similar to the idea presented here. However, the effect of this idea on the final results was not reported.

There are also several works that use synonyms in the target language for improving example alignments. A well-known work of this nature is (Brown 1996).

Phillips et al. (2007) and Cavalli-Sforza and Phillips in Chapter Three of this book present an Arabic-to-English example-based system. Similar to our work, they broaden the way the system performs matching. That system matches words based on their morphological information, so as to obtain more relevant chunks that could not otherwise be found. It showed some improvement over state-of-the-art example-based Arabic-to-English translation systems. This matching approach also resulted in additional irrelevant matched fragments, which had to be removed in later stages.

There are a number of works on automatic thesaurus creation. Some of them use parallel corpora for finding semantically-related source-language words based on their translations. Lin and Pantel (2001) extracted paraphrases from a monolingual corpus by measuring the similarity of dependency relationships. They use a syntactical parser to parse every sentence in their corpus and measure the similarity between paths in the dependency parses using mutual information. Paths with high mutual information were defined as paraphrases. Glickman and Dagan (2003) describe an algorithm for finding synonymous verbs in a monolingual corpus. This was also done using a syntax parser for building a vector containing the subject, object and other arguments for every verb they find in their corpus. Later, they use these vectors to find similarities between verbs. Overall, this technique showed competitive results with the one introduced by Lin and Pantel (2001). Nonetheless, since both techniques may perform differently on a given case, they suggested that the methods should be combined to obtain better results.

One interesting work is (Dyvik 2004), which uses an English-Norwegian parallel corpus for building a lattice of semantically-related English and Norwegian words. It then discovers relations such as synonyms and hyponyms. Another related work (van der Plas & Tiedemann 2006) uses a multilingual sentence-aligned parallel corpus for extraction of synonyms, antonyms and hyponyms for Dutch.

Our own work focuses on matching translation examples using various levels of morphological information plus synonyms, keeping the number of matched fragments for the transfer step as low as possible. We also measure the effect of considering the topic of the translation examples and the input sentence by allowing the system to match on the synonym level only if the candidate translation example and the input sentence are about the same topic.

3. System description

3.1 Translation corpus

The translation examples in our system were extracted from a collection of parallel, sentence-aligned, unvocalized Arabic-English documents, taken from a news-related corpus published by the Linguistic Data Consortium (LDC2004T18). All the Arabic translation examples were morphologically analyzed using the Buckwalter morphological analyzer, and then part-of-speech tagged using AMIRA (Diab et al. 2004), in such a way that, for each word, we consider only the relevant morphological analyses with the corresponding part-of-speech tag. Each translation example was aligned on the word level, using the Giza++ (Och & Ney 2003) system, which is an implementation of the IBM word alignment models (Brown et al. 1993). The Arabic version of the corpus was indexed on the word, stem and lemma levels (stem and lemma, as defined by the Buckwalter analyzer). So, for each given Arabic word, we are able to retrieve all translation examples that contain that word on any of those three levels.

3.2 Matching

Given a new input sentence, the system begins by searching the corpus for translation examples for which the Arabic version matches fragments of the input sentence. In the implementation we are describing, the system is restricted to fragmenting the input sentence so that a matched fragment must be a combination of one or more complete adjacent base-phrases of the input sentence. The base-phrases are initially extracted using the AMIRA tool. The same fragment can be found in more than one translation example. Therefore, a *match-score* is assigned to each fragment-translation pair, signifying the quality of the matched fragment in the specific translation example. Fragments are matched word by word, so the score for a fragment is the average of the individual word match-scores. To deal with data sparseness, we generalize the relatively small corpus by matching words on text, stem, lemma, morphological, cardinal, proper-noun and synonym levels, with each level assigned a different score. These match-levels are defined as follows:

Text level means an exact match. It credits the words in the match with the maximum possible score.

Stem level is a match of word stems. For instance, the words الدستورية (*Aldusotuwriyh*, "the constitutionality") and دستوريتي (*dusotuwriytiy*, "my constitutional") share the stem دستوري (*dusotuwriy*). This match-level currently credits words with somewhat less than a text-level match only because we do not have a component that can modify the translation appropriately.

Lemma level matches are words that share a lemma. For instance, the following words match in their lemmas, but not stems: مارق (*maAriq*, "apostate"); مراق (*mur~aAq*, "apostates"). The lemma of a word is found using the Buckwalter analyzer. For the same reasons as stem-level matches, an imperfect match score is assigned in this case. When dealing with unvocalized text, there are, of course, complicated situations when both words have the same unvocalized stem but different lemmas, for example, the words كتب (*katab*, "wrote") and كتب (*kutub*, "books"). Such cases are not yet handled accurately, since we are not working with a context-sensitive Arabic lemmatizer, and so cannot unambiguously determine the correct lemma of an Arabic word. Actually, by "lemma match", we mean that words match on any one of their possible lemmas. Still, the combination of the Buckwalter morphological analyzer and the AMIRA part-of-speech tagger allows us to reduce the number of possible lemmas for every Arabic word, so as to reduce the degree of ambiguity. Further investigation, as well as working with a context-sensitive morphology analyzer (Habash & Rambow 2005), will allow us to better handle such situations.

Cardinal level matches apply to all numeric words. Correcting the translation of the input word is trivial.

Proper-noun level matches are words that are both tagged as proper nouns by the part-of-speech tagger. In most cases, the words are interchangeable and, consequently, the translation can be easily fixed in the transfer step.

Morphological level matches are words that match based only on their morphological features. For example, two nouns that have the definite-article prefix ال (*Al*, "the") at the beginning constitute a morphological match. This is a very weak level, since it basically allows a match of two different words with totally different meanings. In the transfer step, some of the necessary corrections are done, so this level appears, all the same, to be useful when using a large number of translation examples.

Synonym level matches, the additional feature investigated in the current work, are words that are deemed to be synonyms, according to our automatically extracted thesaurus. Since synonyms are considered interchangeable in many cases, this level credits the words with 95%, which is almost the maximum possible. Using a score of 100% reduces translation results because sometimes synonym-based fragments hide other text-based fragments, and the latter are usually more accurate.

At this point in our experiments, we are using ad-hoc match-level scores, with the goal of a qualitative evaluation of the effect of including the synonym level for matching. Exact-text matches and cardinal matches receive full weight (100%); synonyms, just a tad bit less, namely 95%; stems and proper nouns, 90%; lemmas and stems are scored at 80%; morphological matches receive only 40%.

Fragments are stored in a structure comprising the following:

1. source pattern – the fragment's Arabic text, taken from the input sentence;
2. example pattern – the fragment's Arabic text, taken from the matched translation example;
3. example – the English translation of the example pattern;
4. match score – the score computed for the fragment and its example translation.

Fragments with a score below some predefined threshold are discarded, because passing low-score fragments to the next step would dramatically increase the total running time and sometimes make it unfeasible to process all fragments.

4. Noun experiment

In this experiment, we derive noun synonyms and use them in the matching step. Since Arabic WordNet is still under development, we developed an automatic technique for creating a thesaurus for Arabic nouns, using the Buckwalter gloss information, extended with English WordNet relations. Synonyms for verbs were created in a different way, since verbs seem to be more difficult to work with than nouns: the meaning of an Arabic verb usually changes when used with different prepositions. We describe our approach for automatically finding verb synonyms in the next section.

4.1 The noun thesaurus

Every noun stem in the Buckwalter list was compared to all the other stems when looking for synonym relations. Each Buckwalter stem entry provides one or more glosses. Sharing an English translation, however, is insufficient for determining that two stems are synonymous, because of polysemy; we do not know which of a translation's possible senses was intended for any particular stem. Therefore, we need to attempt to determine stem senses automatically. We ask the English WordNet for all (noun) synsets (sets of synonyms) of every English translation of a stem. A synset containing two or more of the Buckwalter translations is taken to be a possible sense for the given stem. This assumption is based on the idea that if a stem has two or more different translations that semantically intersect, it should probably be interpreted as their common meaning. We also consider the hyponym-hypernym relation between the translations' senses and understand a stem to have the sense of the shared hyponym in this case.

Based on the above information, we considered five levels of synonymy for Arabic stems:

Level 1 – two stems have more than one translation in common.

Level 2 – two stems have more than one sense in common, or they have just one sense in common but this sense is shared by all the translations.

Level 3 – each stem has one and the same translation.

Level 4 – each stem has exactly one translation and the two translations are English synonyms.

Level 5 – the stems are co-translations, that is, they have one translation in common.

Every stem pair is assigned the highest possible level of synonymy, or none when none of the above levels applies. The resultant thesaurus contains 22,621 nouns; 20,512 level-1 relations; 1479 relations on level 2; 17,166 on level 3; 38,754 on level 4, and 137,240 on level 5.

The quality of the translation system was tested for each level of synonymy, individually, starting with level 1, then adding level 2 and so forth. Figure 3 shows an example of a relation between two Arabic stems. The stem اعادة (*AçAdħ*, "return") is matched to the stem كرور (*krwr*, "return") on level 2 because the first stem is translated as both "repetition" and "return", which share the same synset. The second stem is translated as "return" and "recurrence", which also share the same synset as the first stem. Therefore level 2 is the highest appropriate one. Table 1 shows some extracted synonyms and their levels.

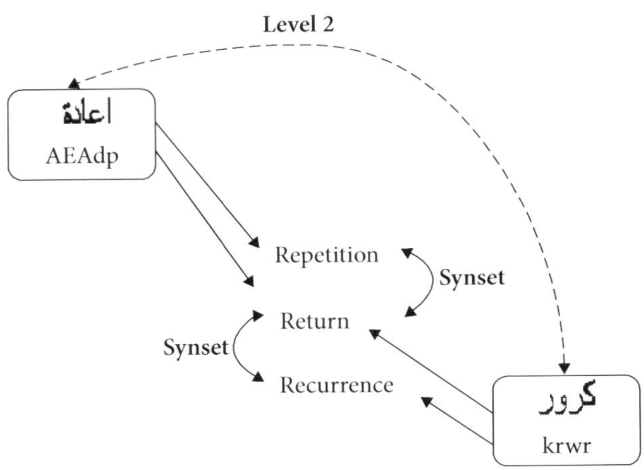

Figure 3. Synonym relation, level-2 example

Table 1. Examples of extracted synonyms

Synonyms	Level
nšyj/dmς ("crying")	4
sTH/sqf/("ceiling")	5
zlςwm/Hlqwm ("throat")	1
njdħ/AςAnħ ("help"; "support")	2
AbtdA'/ftH ("beginning")	5
AxtrAς/AbtkAr ("invention")	3

4.2 Using noun synonyms for translation

The extracted thesaurus was used for matching source language fragments based on synonyms. Finding a synonym for a given word is not a simple task, considering that input sentences are not given with word senses. Matching input words based on synonymy without knowing their true senses is error-prone, because one might match two synonym words based on a specific sense that is not the one used by the author. One way to handle this issue would be to use a word-sense-disambiguation tool for Arabic to uncover the intended sense of each input sentence word. Although there has been some research in this area, we could not find any available tool that produces reasonable results. Even were there one, it would probably use English WordNet senses, since Arabic WordNet is not ready yet.

Another option for matching synonyms is to use the immediate context of a candidate word for matching. Given a pair of words, a window of several words appearing around each may be compared on several WordNet levels and a final score can be computed on that basis. Candidate pairs crossing a predefined threshold can be considered as having the same sense. This direction was left for future investigation.

In this work, we decided to experiment with a different route. We classify each input sentence by topic, as well as all the corpus translation examples. For each translation example, we consider synonyms only if its topic-set intersects with that of the input sentence. The classification was done using the manually-tagged Reuters-21578 corpus for English, since we could not find a similar corpus for Arabic. First, we trained a simple classifier on the training-set given by Reuters, building a statistical model for every topic of the predefined Reuter topic list. We used the support-vector-machine (Joachims 2002) model for this classification task, it having proved to be one of the most appropriate for classification for this corpus. Feature-vectors consisted of *tf-idf* values for English stems, extracted from English WordNet by a morphological analyzer, ignoring stems of stop words. The classifier was tested on 1219 documents from the test-set provided by Reuters, producing accurate results – in the 94% range in most cases.

In the next step, we used this classifier to classify the English half of all the translation examples in our parallel corpus, allowing for more than one topic per document. In addition, the Arabic part of those translation examples was used as a training-set for training another classifier for the same topic list for Arabic. Like its English equivalent, it uses stems as features, ignores the stem of stop words, and creates feature-vectors using the *tf-idf* function. Stems were extracted using the Buckwalter morphological analyzer. The accuracy of this classifier was not measured due to the lack of any manually tagged test-set.

Returning to the translation process: Given a new sentence from an input document, the system begins by classifying the entire input document using the Arabic classifier and determining its topic-set, which is assigned to all sentences within that document. Finally, during the matching step, we allow the system to consider synonyms only in the case of a non-empty intersection of topic-sets of the input sentence and the examined translation example. The efficacy of this classification feature was examined and results show a slight improvement in final translations compared to the same conditions running without classification. We elaborate further on this in the results section.

4.3 Experimental results

Experiments were conducted on two corpora. The first contains 29,992 (1,247,468 Arabic words) translation examples and the second one contains 58,115 (1,997,434 Arabic words). The system was tested on all levels of synonyms relations and the effect of using the classification feature on every level was examined.

The following results are based on a test set of 586 sentences from 68 documents (17370 words) taken from the 2009 NIST MT Evaluation data and compared to four reference translations. We evaluated the results under some of the common automatic criteria for machine-translation evaluation: BLEU (Papineni 2002) and METEOR (Banerjee & Lavie 2005). Table 2 shows some experimental results, presented as BLEU and METEOR scores.

From these results, one can observe that, in general, the system performs slightly better when using synonyms. The most prominent improvement in the BLEU score was achieved when using all levels, 1 through 5, on the small corpus. However, the same experiments using the large corpus did not show significant improvements. This was expected: the larger corpus has more translation examples that match more fragments exactly. Using synonyms at level 5 caused reductions in all scores in the large corpora. This is probably because level 5 gives synonyms

Table 2. Experimental results – BLEU and METEOR (MTOR) scores

Test	Small corpus				Large corpus			
	w/classification		w/o classification		w/classification		w/o classification	
	BLEU	MTOR	BLEU	MTOR	BLEU	MTOR	BLEU	MTOR
Level 1	0.1186	0.4748	0.1176	0.4756	0.1515	0.5183	0.1506	0.5185
Levels 1–2	0.1176	0.4769	0.1173	0.4748	0.1515	0.5183	0.1505	0.5186
Levels 1–3	0.1186	0.4762	0.1176	0.4770	0.1520	0.5186	0.1510	0.5189
Levels 1–4	0.1187	0.1179	0.1179	0.4756	0.1519	0.5184	0.1509	0.5188
Levels 1–5	**0.1192** (+9%)	0.4746	0.1177	0.4751	0.1500	0.5181	0.1484	0.5170
No synonym			0.1084	0.4460			0.1485	0.5194

of low confidence, thereby introducing errors in matching corpus fragments, which may hide better fragments that could have participated in the output translation. On the other hand, when using level 5 synonyms on the small corpus, the system performed even better than when not using them. That can be explained by the fact that the small corpus probably produces fewer fragments, and the ones based on synonyms can cover ranges of the input sentence that were not covered by other fragments. However, when using the classification feature over the large corpus, the system was able to remove some of the problematic fragments, resulting in better scores.

In general, when synonyms are used and contribute significantly, this classification feature did show some improvement. We can also see that experiments in which synonyms did not help improve translations significantly show a reduction in final scores when using classification. This strengthens our intuition that real synonyms are more likely to be found in documents dealing with similar subject matters. We expect that taking the words' local context into consideration, as mentioned above, would result in even better performance.

In addition to the traditional automatic evaluation for the resulted translations, we have measured the effect of using synonyms on the corpus coverage. Table 3 summarizes the number of uncovered 1–4 grams when using synonyms vs. without using synonyms on the small corpus. The results show that when using synonyms the system was able to find an additional 252 bigrams; however, on longer n-grams the system did not show significant improvement. As expected, increasing the size of the corpus reduced the positive effect on n-gram coverage.

Table 3. Experimental results – uncovered n-grams in the small corpus

	w/synonyms	w/o synonyms
Unigrams	733	738
Bigrams	7612 (+3.2%)	7864
Trigrams	11554	11632
4-grams	11224	11243

5. Verb experiment

For the second experiment, we extract Arabic verb synonyms using a corpus of comparable documents. The evaluation of this process was performed both manually and automatically. As in the noun experiment, we measure the translation quality of a system that uses the extracted synonyms in the matching step. In the next phase, we will extend our work for the purpose of finding longer equivalents, also known as *paraphrases*, extracted from the same comparable corpora.

5.1 The verb thesaurus

We chose to use comparable documents rather than a monolingual or parallel corpus for finding Arabic verb synonyms. Existing parallel corpora for Arabic are usually translated to English, and since we currently focus on the Arabic-to-English direction, any additional parallel corpus could have been preprocessed by a translation system in the usual way. The contribution of additional equivalents that were extracted from a parallel corpus, which is loaded into the system in the traditional way, is expected to be very limited. However, we could use other parallel corpora, which pair Arabic with other languages, allowing us to use the other language as a pivot and find paraphrases in cases where two Arabic phrases share the same translation. Bannard and Callison-Burch (2005) implemented this idea using parallel corpora of French and Spanish paired with other languages. However, the parallel corpora we could find so far that pair Arabic with languages other than English contain a very limited quantity of sentences, which makes it irrelevant for the synonym extraction task. Since Arabic is one of the UN official languages, we could have built such corpora using the formal published documentation by the UN, provided in seven different languages. Using the same algorithm implemented by Bannard and Callison-Burch on automatically sentence-aligned Arabic and the other six UN languages is something that we consider trying in the near future.

On the other hand, a large monolingual corpus is easy to obtain, but the context of candidate pairs is undefined. To overcome this problem, in most of the cases, a full syntax parser is used to find relevant syntactic features for describing the context of a possible synonym match. This fact limits the language set of such an algorithm. Moreover, the lack of an indication of context forces the algorithm to be more restrictive when trying to match a potential candidate, usually resulting in fewer extracted synonyms. However, using syntax dependency information helps in the identification of discontinuous synonyms, which are very common in Arabic.

Our corpus was derived from the Arabic Gigaword corpus. Among all articles published by two news agencies (al-Nahar and al-Hayat) on the same dates, we took only those whose titles matched lexically. The matching criterion was simple: for every candidate pair of articles, we count the number of matched stems (using a morphological analyzer for Arabic) appearing in their titles and for each single article we choose another article having the largest number of matched stems to be its match. For the time being, we eliminated cases in which one article matched more than one document. Currently, we have only created a small corpus, which is being used in the development steps.

We based our ideas on the work of Barzilay and McKeown (2001) on paraphrasing in English. The first task is to obtain a (partial) word alignment of every document pair. Since they used various English translations of the same source, the alignment could be obtained with less effort. This is not the case when using a corpus of comparable documents as a source for synonym extraction. Documents that deal with the same event are not necessarily a translation of the same source, thus finding sentence alignments is impossible. Therefore, we decided to align together every verb pair sharing the same stem. Obviously, many-to-many alignment is also possible. In addition to this initial alignment, we created a list of potential synonym relations for a large list of Arabic verbs. This list was extracted using the English glosses provided with the Arabic stem list of the Buckwalter morphological analyzer, exactly as was done in the noun experiment using the English WordNet. In this case, stems that share at least one translation in common or whose translations are English synonyms were deemed to be synonyms. This is equivalent to taking all the synonyms of level 5 as defined in the noun experiment. Unlike nouns, Arabic verbs tend to change their senses with different attached prepositions; therefore, the extracted list of synonymous verbs is error-prone. Note that Buckwalter's stem list does not contain prepositional information, so this list cannot be treated as a thesaurus at all, but it will be used in a different way by our extraction algorithm.

Given the initial alignment for every document pair within the corpus, we start to look for those *contexts* in which verb synonyms exist (at this stage, only similar verbs). A context is defined as a list of features extracted from the *n* (*n*, a parameter, determines the context size) words on the left and right sides of the verb within the sentence and mainly contains morpho-syntactic information. The features that we intend to use are the word's stem (since Arabic is a highly inflectional language) and part-of-speech tags, estimated automatically by AMIRA. Figure 4 shows an example for a verb context when *n*=2.

Sentence 1:
mktb Alsnywrp wdywAn Âwlmrt ***ynfyAn*** *xbrA ςn lqA' fy šrm Alšyx.*

Translation:
Seniora's office and Olmert's administration deny a story about a meeting in Sharm al-Sheikh.

Sentence 2:
mktb Alsnywrħ ***ynfy*** *xbrA ςn lqAyĥ mswŵlyn AšrAyŷlyyn.*

Translation:
Seniora's office denies a story about a meeting with Israeli officials.

Verb: *nfy* (*ynfyAn, ynfy*)

Context:
Left-1: (NN, NNP) Right-1: (NN$_1$, IN$_2$)
Left-2: (NN, NNP) Right-2: (NN$_1$, IN$_2$)

Figure 4. An example of a context

In this example, the verb *nfy* ("deny") appears in the first sentence in its imperfect dual form, while in the second sentence it is in its imperfect singular form. The stems are not used as direct features, but only to indicate equality of words located in both context parts. In such a case, the part-of-speech tag will contain the index of the matched word in the other part of the context, as can be seen in this example: On the right-hand side, the two following words (*xbrA*, *ςn*) are exactly the same; however, on the left hand side there are no stem-based similar words.

We will consider adding other features. Matching context content words (not functional) based on a direct WordNet hypernym relation is possible. In such cases we will match the Arabic equivalents of "blue" and "green" as both words being part of synsets with direct hyponym relation to the same synset, namely, color. The main challenge here is the lack of a robust and extensive WordNet for Arabic. Instead, we will use the English WordNet for the gloss entries of the words' stem.

Arabic verbs often use additional particles to highlight their objects. Different particles can completely change the meaning of the verb. For instance, the meaning of the direct-object version of the transitive verb *qDy* is "to judge" and the meaning of the same verb using the preposition *ςly* to mark the object is "put an end to".

Therefore, we should also use the word that appears right after the first preposition as part of the context.

Although parsing Arabic text is a difficult task, there have been recent works on dependency parsing in Arabic that we will consider using to locate the subject and object of each verb and then consider them as the context, instead of choosing the immediate words surrounding the verb. Arabic sentences are often written with many noun and verb modifiers and descriptors, so we think that using such a parser will help produce more accurate synonyms.

Based on the ideas of Barzilay and McKeown (2001), we can identify the best contexts using the strength and frequency of each context, where the strength of a positive context is defined as p/N and the strength of a negative context is defined as n/N, where p is the number of times the context appears in a positive example (similar verbs), n is the number of times it appears in a negative example (non-similar verbs), and N is simply the frequency of the context in the entire corpus. We then select the most frequent k positive and negative contexts (k, a parameter) whose strength is higher than a predefined threshold and use them for extracting synonymous verbs. We do this by finding all instances of each selected positive context that are not covered by a negative context in every document pair. The verbs that are surrounded by those contexts are deemed synonymous. Since we do not use word alignment of any kind, finding negative examples seems to be non-trivial. For this reason, we previously created the potential synonym verb list. In every document pair, we look for verb-pair candidates, which are not even synonyms on the potential list. Such verb pairs are marked as negative examples.

To evaluate this process, we examine a random number of the resultant synonyms with their extracted contexts. Callison-Burch et al. (2008) proposed ParaMetric, an automatic metric for measuring paraphrasing techniques. The evaluation in this setting is done using manually word-aligned groups of sentences in which sentences are translations of the same source. This gold-standard set was used to test different paraphrasing techniques, calculating the relative recall and the lower bound precision of each one of them. However, this was done based on a corpus of multiple English translations of the same Chinese texts, which was made to serve machine translation evaluation campaigns. Unfortunately, there is no similar corpus available for Arabic, so for the time being at least we have had to abandon this direction.

An expert will evaluate our results by examining some number of pairs, given along with the contexts in which they were found, and decide whether the verbs are synonyms (at least in one context) or non-synonyms (wrongly identified as synonyms in all the given contexts). We want to measure the precision and relative recall, based on manually tagging paraphrase relations between all candidate pairs within a limited set of compared documents.

5.2 Using synonyms in translation

As in the previous experiment, we allow the system to find matches on a synonym level. As before, the evaluation of this process was done automatically using the common metrics (BLEU, METEOR). Some features were tested for their effect on the final results separately. (In this experiment, we did not check the effect of using a topic classifier as a tool for deciding when synonyms should be considered and when they should not.)

Since the automatic metrics may hide the improvement of using paraphrases in the internal matching step, we also performed a manual evaluation. An expert evaluated a predefined small test-set. The expert scored the synonym-based extracted patterns, given with their contexts. First, the source-language part corresponding to the input sentence fragment was examined, and then the quality of the translations was.

5.3 Experimental results

We use 5500 document pairs, extracted from the Arabic Gigaword. The total number of words is about three million. The context window that we used is of size 2. That is, we consider all the possible contexts surrounding a verb with the limitation of one or two words before the candidate verbs and after. The strength threshold for selecting the best contexts of both categories is 0.95, as suggested by Barizlay and McKeown, and the number of best contexts (defined as k above) we use is 20. (We found that, $k = 10$, as used by Barzilay and McKeown, is too restrictive in our settings, and that, therefore, the result set was relatively small).

Two experts evaluated the resultant verb pairs. The verb pairs were given along with the different contexts in which they were found. For each candidate pair, each expert was requested to make one of the following decisions: *correct* – verb instances are exchanged in some contexts; or *incorrect* – verb instances are not exchangeable at all. There needed to be at least one context in which a verb pair is semantically replaceable in order for them to be marked as correct paraphrases by the experts. They were also allowed to say that verbs are correct paraphrases even if their meaning is modified by another word in the context. Recall that the system was instructed to identify whether two verbs have the same meaning in a given context. Therefore, it decides so even if the meaning is defined by an expression of more than one word, including the target verb. Table 4 shows the expert decisions.

Table 4. Experts' evaluation

Unique candidates	Unique synonyms	Expert 1: Correct synonyms	Expert 2: Correct synonyms
15,101	139	120 (86% precision)	103 (74% precision)

In all, we found about 15,000 unique (based on the verbs' lemmas) candidates. Of these, the classifier decided that only 139 are synonyms. While 120 were found to be correct by the first expert, the second expert found only 103 to be correct, yielding precision values of 86% and 74%, respectively. Since we do not know how many of the 15,000 candidates are actually synonyms, we have not calculated recall. Table 5 shows some synonym examples that were extracted by this technique and Table 6 shows two of the best contexts for the positive candidates.

Table 5. Examples of extracted synonyms

Synonyms
Ǎçtql/Âwqf ("arrest")
bθ~/nq~l ("broadcast")
Ǎstqbl/Ǎltqy ("meet")

Table 6. Some of the best contexts for the positive candidates

Best contexts
Left-1: (NN0) Right-1: (IN, NN) Left-2: (NN0) Right-2: (IN)
Left-1: (NN, WP0) Right-1: (NN0) Left-2: (WP1) Right-2: (NN0)

Once we found the abovementioned synonyms, we used them in translation, under settings similar to those described in the noun experiment. In this case, we tested the system only using the corpus containing about 1.2 million Arabic words and on the same test-set: 586 sentences from 68 documents (17370 words) taken from the 2009 NIST MT Evaluation data comparing to four reference translations. We automatically evaluated the results under BLEU and realized that there was only a slight insignificant improvement in the final results. We decided to examine the results manually, this time it was done only by the first author. Overall, we found 193 input sentence fragments for which at least one of the words matched on a synonym level. For simplicity, we will call these *syn-fragments*. For 162 syn-fragments, the synonym matching is correct under the sentence context. Out of these syn-fragments, 57 are covering parts in the input sentence that are not covered by other fragments of at least the same size. That means they might help to better cover the input sentence in the matching step, however our current recombination algorithm was not able to capture that. We further looked at the extracted translation for the 193 syn-fragments and found that only 97 were actually translated correctly. All the other syn-fragments received wrong translations by the system. At first glance, in most cases, the synonyms were not the main reason for the wrong translation. It seems more like the traditional problem of error-prone word alignment affecting the translation of the fragments. Of the 63 syn-fragments that participated in the final translations, only 42 were translated correctly. Seeing these results, one can conclude that, unsurprisingly, the system is making bad choices when it tries to select the best fragments for incorporation in the final translations. Remember that our current example-based system is using a very simple recombination technique, and it still needs to be adapted to use a more standard model. That can explain why we could not see a real improvement in BLEU score.

6. Conclusions

The system we are working on has demonstrated a promising potential for using contextual synonyms in an example-based approach to machine translation, for Arabic, in particular. We found that noun synonyms benefit from being matched carefully by considering the topic of the sentence in which they appear. Comparing other ways of using context to properly match the true senses of ambiguous synonyms is definitely a direction for future investigation.

Another interesting observation is the fact that using synonyms on a large corpus did not result in a significant improvement of the final results, as it did for a smaller corpus. This suggests that synonyms can contribute to EBMT for language pairs lacking large parallel corpora, by enabling the system to better exploit the small number of examples in the given corpus.

More work is still needed for better aligning the translation examples. Sometimes, even if the system succeeds in matching examples based on synonyms, the final translation was wrong due to a sparse alignment table for the retrieved translation example.

Of course, smoothing out the output translations is an essential step toward understanding the real potential of our system. This step is currently being investigated and planned for implementation in the near future.

Though the standard scores achieved by our system remain low, primarily because of the above-mentioned alignment and smoothing issues, a detailed examination of numerous translations suggests that the benefits of using matches based on synonyms will carry over to more complete translation systems. What is true for our automatically-generated thesaurus is even more likely to hold when a quality Arabic thesaurus will become available for mechanical use. In the meanwhile, we will continue working on different methods for automatic extraction of semantic equivalents for Arabic.

As demonstrated in the verb experiment, the classifier, which was trained to find new verb synonyms in a corpus of comparable documents, performs pretty well in terms of precision. Even though we have not yet calculated the recall, by manually looking over the candidates, we could see some that there are true synonyms that were not yet discovered. We are now working on different techniques for building a new classifier for extracting semantic equivalents from a corpus of comparable documents. We even plan to consider more context features, such as marking words that are derived from the same WordNet type. A dependency parser seems to be a powerful tool for finding equivalents. Had we had one, we could have used the subject and the object phrases as the context of the verbs rather than using a fixed-size surrounding window.

The two experiments described here are just first steps toward the larger goal of deriving longer paraphrases for Arabic and using them to improve machine translation.

References

Banerjee, S., and A. Lavie. 2005. Meteor: An automatic metric for MT evaluation with improved correlation with human judgments. In *Proceedings of the 43rd Annual ACL Meeting. Workshop on Intrinsic and Extrinsic Evaluation Measures for MT and/or Summarization*, 65–72. Ann Arbor MI.

Bannard, C., and C. Callison-Burch. 2005. Paraphrasing with bilingual parallel corpora. In *Proceedings of the Annual Meeting of the Association of Computational Linguistics (ACL 2005)*, 597–604. Ann Arbor MI.

Bar, K., and N. Dershowitz. 2010. Using synonyms for Arabic-to-English example-based translation. In *Proceedings of the Ninth Conference of the Association for Machine Translation in the Americas (AMTA 9)*. Denver CO.

Barzilay, R., and K. McKeown. 2001. Extracting paraphrases from a parallel corpus. In *Proceedings of the Annual Meeting of the Association of Computational Linguistics (ACL 2001)*, 50–57. Toulouse, France.

Brown, P. F., Pietra, S. A. D., Pietra, V. J. D., and Mercer, R. L. (1993). The mathematics of statistical machine translation. Computational Linguistics, 19(2): 263–313.

Brown, R. D. 1996. Example-based machine translation in the Pangloss system. In *Proceedings of International Conference on Computational Linguistics (COLING-96)*, Vol. 1, 169–174. Copenhagen, Denmark.

Brown, R. D. 1999. Adding linguistic knowledge to a lexical example-based translation system. In *Proceedings of the International Conference on Theoretical and Methodological Issues in Machine Translation (TMI)*, 22–32. Chester, UK.

Buckwalter, T. 2002. *Buckwalter Arabic Morphological Analyzer Version 1.0.* Linguistic Data Consortium, Philadelphia PA.

Callison-Burch, C. 2007. Paraphrasing and Translation. Ph.D dissertation, University of Edinburgh.

Callison-Burch, C., T. Cohn, and M. Lapata. 2008. ParaMetric: An automatic evaluation metric for paraphrasing. In *Proceedings of the 22nd International Conference on Computational Linguistics (COLING 2008)*, 97–104.

Diab, M., K. Hacioglu, and D. Jurafsky. 2004. *Automatic Tagging of Arabic Text: From Raw Text to Base Phrase Chunks.* The National Science Foundation, Washington DC.

Dyvik H. 2004. Translations as semantic mirrors: From parallel corpus to WordNet. *Language and Computers* 49 (1): 311–326.

Glickman, O., and I. Dagan. 2003. Identifying lexical paraphrases from a single corpus: A case study for verbs. In *Proceedings of the Recent Advantages in Natural Language Processing (RANLP-03)*, 81–90.

Joachims, T. 2002. *Learning to Classify Text Using Support Vector Machines.* Dordrecht: Kluwer.

Habash, N., and O. Rambow. 2005. Arabic tokenization, morphological analysis, and part-of-speech tagging in one fell swoop. In *Proceedings of the Conference of American Association for Computational Linguistics*, 578–580. Ann Arbor MI.

Lee, Y.-S. 2004. Morphological analysis for statistical machine translation. In *Proceedings of Human Language Technologies: The Annual Conference of the North American Chapter of the Association for Computational Linguistics (HLT-NAACL-04)*, 57–60. Lisbon, Portugal.

van der Plas. L., and J. Tiedemann. 2006. Finding synonyms using automatic word alignment and measures of distributional similarity. In *Proceedings of the Annual Meeting of the Association for Computational Linguistics and International Conference on Computational Linguistics (COLING/ACL 2006), Main Conference Poster Sessions*, 866–873.

Maruyama, H., and H. Watanabe. 1992. Tree cover search algorithm for example-based translation. In *Proceedings of the 4th International Conference on Theoretical and Methodological Issues in Machine Translation (TMI)*, 173–184.

Nagao, M. 1984. A framework of mechanical translation between Japanese and English by analogy principle. In *Artificial and Human Intelligence.* Alick Elithorn & Rana Banerji (eds), 173–180. Amsterdam: North-Holland.

Nakazawa, T., K. Yu, D. Kawahara, and S. Kurohashi. 2006. Example-based machine translation based on deeper NLP. In *Proceedings of International Workshop on Spoken Language Translation (IWSLT'06)*, 64–70. Kyoto, Japan.

Nirenburg, S., S. Beale, and C. Domashnev. 1994. A full-text experiment in example-based machine translation. In *Proceedings of the International Conference on New Methods in Language Processing (NeMLaP)*, 78–87. Manchester, UK.

Lin, D., and P. Pantel. 2001. Discovery of inference rules for question answering. *Natural Language Engineering* 7(4): 343–36.

Papineni, K., S. Roukos, T. Ward, and W.-J. Zhu. 2002. BLEU: A method for automatic evaluation of machine translation. In *Proceedings of the 40th Annual Meeting of the Association for Computational Linguistics (ACL)*, 311–318. Philadelphia PA.

Phillips, A. B., V. Cavalli-Sforza, and R. D. Brown. 2007. Improving example-based machine translation through morphological generalization and adaptation. In *Proceedings of Machine Translation Summit XI*, Copenhagen, 369–375. Denmark.

Sadat, F., and N. Habash. 2006. Arabic preprocessing schemes for statistical machine translation. In *Proceedings of Human Language Technology Conference of the NAACL*, 49–52. New York NY.

Sato, S., and M. Nagao. 1990. Toward memory-based translation. In *Proceedings of the 13th International Conference on Computational Linguistics (COLING)*, Vol. 3, 247–252.

Stroppa, N., D. Groves, K. Sarasola, and A. Way. 2006. Example-based machine translation of the Basque language. In *Proceedings 7th Conference of the Association for Machine Translation in the Americas*, 232–241.

Sumita, E., and H. Iida. 1995. Heterogeneous computing for example-based translation of spoken language. In *Proceedings of the International Conference on Theoretical and Methodological Issues in Machine Translation (TMI)*, 273–286.

Arabic preprocessing for Statistical Machine Translation

Schemes, techniques and combinations

Nizar Habash & Fatiha Sadat
Center for Computational Learning Systems, Columbia University /
Department of Computer Science, Université du Québec á Montréal

Arabic is a morphologically rich language. This poses some problems for statistical machine translation (SMT) approaches. In this chapter, we study the effect of different Arabic word-level preprocessing schemes and techniques on the quality of phrase-based SMT. We also present and evaluate different methods for combining preprocessing schemes. Our results show that given large training data sets, splitting off proclitics only performs best. However, for small training data sets, it is best to apply English-like tokenization using part-of-speech tags, and sophisticated morphological analysis and disambiguation. Moreover, choosing the appropriate preprocessing scheme produces a significant increase in BLEU score if there is a change in genre between training and test data. We also found that combining different preprocessing schemes leads to improved translation quality.

1. Introduction

Statistical machine translation (SMT) is quite robust when it comes to the choice of input representation. It only requires consistency between training and testing. As a result, there is a wide range of possible preprocessing choices for data used in SMT. This is even more so for morphologically rich languages such as Arabic. We use the term "preprocessing" to describe various input modifications applied to raw training and testing texts for SMT. Preprocessing includes different kinds of tokenization, stemming, part-of-speech (POS) tagging and lemmatization. The ultimate goal of preprocessing is to improve the quality of the SMT output by addressing issues such as training data sparsity. We refer to a specific kind of preprocessing as a "scheme" and differentiate it from the "technique" used to obtain it.

Since we wish to study the effect of word-level preprocessing, we do not utilize any syntactic information (see Chapter 7 on the use of syntax). Of course, for a morphologically rich language like Arabic the boundary between syntax and morphology can be fuzzy. We define the word (and by extension its morphology) to be limited to strings separated by white space, punctuation and numbers. Thus, some prepositional particles and conjunctions are considered part of word morphology.

In this chapter, we present a definition of the space of possible word-level preprocessing decisions that can be done for Arabic. We report on an extensive study of the effect of several preprocessing schemes on SMT quality. These schemes are evaluated against three different techniques that vary in linguistic complexity; and across a learning curve of training sizes. We also investigate the effect of scheme/technique combination on genre variation between training and testing. Finally, we describe and evaluate different methods for combining preprocessing schemes.

Our results are as follows: (a) for large training data sets, splitting off only conjunctions, prepositions and pre-verbal particles performs best; (b) for small training data sets, following an English-like tokenization and using part-of-speech tags performs best; (c) suitable choice of preprocessing yields an important increase in BLEU score (Papineni et al. 2002) if there is little training data, and/or there is a change in genre between training and test data; (d) sophisticated morphological analysis and disambiguation help significantly in the absence of large data sets; and finally, (e) combining systems using different schemes at the target level, the phrase-table level or both improves MT performance.

The Arabic variety we work with here is Modern Standard Arabic (MSA). The learning-curve experiments we conducted are intended to shed light on how other forms of Arabic, such as Arabic dialects, would behave given their scarce resources. We do not report on any additional forms of preprocessing in this chapter, e.g. no special handling of numbers, dates or by-lines. This is intended to isolate the effect of the phenomena we study so that others can replicate our work. As a result, the BLEU scores we report appear lower than the state-of-the-art reported in the latest National Institute of Standards and Technology (NIST) MT Evaluations.[1] However, we believe the insights learned here are applicable to other phrase-based SMT systems.

Section 2 presents previous relevant research. Section 3 presents some relevant background on Arabic linguistics to motivate the schemes discussed in Section 4. Section 5 presents the tools and data sets used, along with the results of our experiments. Section 6 presents different combination approaches that maximize the use of different schemes.

1. http://www.itl.nist.gov/iad/mig/tests/mt/

2. Related work

Since the inception of SMT in the early 1990s, it was clear that the type of preprocessing done on a parallel corpus has a big impact on translation quality. One of the earliest SMT systems, Candide (Berger et al. 1994), included a fair amount of morpho-syntactic preprocessing to manipulate French text into looking similar to English text. This included word segmentation, morphological analysis and word reordering. The anecdotal intuition in the field is that reduction of word sparsity often improves translation quality. This reduction can be achieved by increasing training data or via morphologically driven preprocessing (Goldwater & McClosky 2005). Different languages and even language pairs may require different treatments. Nießen & Ney (2004) studied the impact of various types of morpho-syntactic restructuring on German-English SMT. This included reattaching separable particles to their verbs, and selective POS tagging of highly ambiguous words. Their investigation in word segmentation showed less benefit than the more sophisticated syntactic manipulation. The effect of splitting words into stems and suffixes has also been studied for other languages: Spanish, Catalan and Serbian (Popovic & Ney 2004). Their results show significant error reduction especially for Serbian, which had fewer resources than the two other languages they studied.

More research is ongoing for languages with more complex morphologies such as Czech. Goldwater & McClosky (2005) show that incorporating various methods of morphological information in Czech-English SMT improves translation quality especially when the different methods are combined. The techniques they use include lemmatization and highlighting features as attached or separated tokens. The data they work with is smaller than other language pairs: it is around 20K sentence pairs drawn from the Prague Czech-English Dependency Treebank (Čmejrek et al. 2004). However, this data is quite rich in that it is manually fully disambiguated. Such a resource is not available to many other languages. Similarly, in this chapter, we investigate the effect of lemmatization on Arabic and the use of different POS tags. We also investigate the effect of Arabic automatic disambiguation.

Specifically on Arabic, Lee (2004) investigated the use of automatic alignment of POS tagged English and affix-stem segmented Arabic to determine whether affixes should be kept separate, deleted or reattached to stems. She also investigated the use of some shallow syntactic knowledge (base phrase chunking) to determine when the Arabic definite article +ال *Al* + 'the' is kept or deleted. Her results show that morphological preprocessing helps but only for the smaller corpora sizes she investigated. As size increases, the benefits diminish. Similarly, Zollmann et al. (2006) used techniques that select appropriate word segmentations in Arabic based on contextual relationships in English. Their techniques lead to improved results. El Isbihani et al. (2006), Riesa & Yarowsky (2006) and de Gispert (2006) apply different levels of morphological preprocessing that also show improvements in Arabic-English SMT. Yang et al. (2007) presented a semi-supervised learning approach that utilizes a heuristic model for learning morpheme segmentation for Arabic dialects and yields some increase in BLEU scores. Other research on preprocessing Arabic suggests that minimal preprocessing, such as splitting off the conjunction +و *w+* 'and', produces best results with very large training data (Och 2005). Elming & Habash (2007) used a variety of tokenization schemes for Arabic to improve results in the task of automatic alignment; however, these improvements did not help MT as much.

System combination for MT has also been investigated by different researchers. Approaches to combination generally either select one of the hypotheses produced by the different systems combined (Nomoto 2004; Paul et al. 2005; Lee 2005) or combine lattices/n-best lists from the different systems with different degrees of synthesis or mixing (Frederking & Nirenburg 1994; Bangalore et al. 2001; Jayaraman & Lavie 2005; Matusov et al. 2006). These different approaches use various translation and language models in addition to other models such as word matching, sentence and document alignment, system translation confidence, phrase translation lexicons, etc.

Finally, the impact of Arabic tokenization has been studied for a variety of NLP tasks particularly information retrieval (Larkey et al. 2007) but also co-reference resolution (Zitouni et al. 2005).

It is hard to compare results to other published research since different corpora, corpora sizes and additional preprocessing are used. The closest previous work we can compare to is Lee (2004). Although she studied different sizes of corpora, our results are comparable to hers in terms of BLEU score and consistent in terms of conclusions. We do, however, select schemes for comparison that are inspired by previous work on Arabic and other languages (Section 4). We extend previous work by studying the effect of morphological disambiguation (beyond POS tagging) on preprocessing and comparing eleven different preprocessing schemes under learning curve conditions and genre variation. We also explore and evaluate various scheme-combination approaches to produce better results. This chapter combines and extends two previously published conference papers which first presented the ideas and results discussed here (Habash & Sadat 2006; Sadat & Habash 2006). The impact of this work can be seen in the number of efforts that follow and extend on the techniques we proposed for Arabic-English SMT (Bender et al. 2007; de Gispert et al. 2009; Bertoldi et al. 2009; Diehl et al. 2009), and more recently for MT from English into Arabic (Badr et al. 2008; El Kholy & Habash 2010a;

Kholy & Habash 2010b; Al-Haj & Lavie 2010). A more detailed discussion of preprocessing for English-Arabic MT appears in Chapter 6.

3. Arabic linguistic issues

Arabic is a morphologically complex language with a large set of morphological features (Habash 2010). We discuss a subset of Arabic linguistic challenges necessary as background for this chapter.

3.1 Orthographic ambiguity

The form of certain letters in Arabic script allows suboptimal orthographic variants of the same word to coexist in the same text. For example, variants of Hamzated Alif, أ *Â* or إ *Ǎ*, are often written without their Hamza (ء *'*) thus appearing like an Alif ا *A*. Also, the Ta-Marbuta (ة *ħ*), which is a morpheme often used as a feminine ending, is sometimes written without its distinctive dots; thus it looks like the letter Ha (ه *h*). Particularly in Egyptian Press, the word final occurrences of the letter Ya (ي *y*) are written dotless, thus resembling an Alif Maqsura (ى *ý*). These variant spellings increase the ambiguity of words. The Arabic script employs diacritics for representing short vowels and doubled consonants. These diacritics are almost always absent in running text, which increases word ambiguity.[2] We preprocess all of our training and evaluation texts to remove all diacritics.

3.2 Clitics

Arabic has a set of attachable clitics to be distinguished from inflectional features such as gender, number, person, voice, aspect, etc. These clitics are written attached to the word and thus increase the ambiguity of alternative readings. We can classify three degrees of cliticization that are applicable to a word base in a strict order:

[CONJ+ [PART+ [Al+ BASE +PRON]]]

At the deepest level, the BASE can have a definite article (+ال *Al+* 'the') or a member of the class of pronominal enclitics, +PRON, (e.g. هم+ *+hm* 'their/them'). Pronominal enclitics can attach to nouns (as possessives) or verbs and prepositions (as objects). The definite article doesn't apply to verbs or prepositions. +PRON and Al+ cannot co-exist on nouns. Next comes the class of particle proclitics

2. In the Penn Arabic Treebank (Maamouri et al. 2004), 1.6% of all words have at least one diacritic indicated by their author (Habash 2010).

(PART+): +ل *l+* 'to/for', +ب *b+* 'by/with', +ك *k+* 'as/such' and +س *s+* 'will/future'. *b+* and *k+* are only nominal; *s+* is only verbal and *l+* applies to both nouns and verbs. At the shallowest level of attachment we find the conjunctions (CONJ+) +و *w+* 'and' and +ف *f+* 'so'. They can attach to everything.

3.3 Adjustment rules

Concatenative morphemes are not always simply attached to a word base. Additional morphological, phonological and orthographic rules are applied to the word. An example of a morphological rule is the feminine morpheme, ة+ *+ħ*, which keeps its form only in word-final positions. In medial position, it is turned into ت+ *+t*. For example, مكتبة+هم *mktbħ+hm* appears as مكتبتهم *mktbthm* 'their library'. An example of an orthographic rule is the deletion of the Alif (ا *A*) of the definite article +ال *Al+* 'the' in nouns when preceded by the preposition +ل *l+* 'to/for' but not with any other prepositional proclitic: e.g., ل+ال+مكتبة *l+Al+mktbħ* 'to the library' is written as للمكتبة *llmktbħ* not as لالمكتبة* **lAlmktbħ*.

3.4 Templatic inflections

Some of the inflectional features in Arabic words are realized templatically by applying a different pattern to the Arabic root. As a result, extracting the lexeme (or lemma) of an Arabic word is not always an easy task and often requires the use of a morphological analyzer. One common example in Arabic nouns is Broken Plurals. For example, the Arabic word كاتب *kAtb* 'writer' has two broken plural forms كتّاب *ktAb* and كتبة *ktbħ* 'writers'. An alternative non-broken plural (concatenatively derived) is كاتبون *kAtbwn* 'writers'. These phenomena highlight two issues related to the task at hand (preprocessing): First, ambiguity in Arabic words is an important issue to address. To determine whether a clitic (or feature) should be split off (or abstracted off) requires that we determine that said feature is indeed present in the word we are considering in context – and not just that it is possible given an analyzer out of context. Secondly, once a specific analysis is determined, the process of splitting off or abstracting off a feature must be clear on what the form of the resulting word should be. In principle, we would like to eliminate adjustments that depend on the missing feature. This ensures reduced sparsity and reduced unnecessary ambiguity. For example, the word كتبتهم *ktbthm* has two possible readings (among others)[3] as 'their writers' or 'I wrote them'. Splitting off the pronominal enclitic +هم *+hm* without normalizing the ت *t* to ة ħ in the nominal

3. The SAMA morphological analyzer produces eight readings: three are cases variants of 'their writers [nominative/accusative/]', four are subject variants of the verb to write (as in 'I/you/she wrote them') and one is a proper noun reading: ك+تبت+هم 'like their Tibet'.

reading leads the coexistence of two forms of the noun كتبة *ktbh* and كتبت *ktbt*. This increased sparsity is only worsened by the fact that the second form is also the verbal form (thus increased ambiguity). More details on Arabic morphology and statistical MT are available in (Habash 2007).

4. Preprocessing: Schemes and techniques

We distinguish between preprocessing techniques and preprocessing schemes: a scheme is a specification of the form of preprocessed output; whereas a technique is the method used to create such output. Given Arabic's morphological complexity, the number of possible preprocessing schemes is very large since any subset of morphological and orthographic features can be separated, deleted or normalized in various ways. To implement any preprocessing scheme, a preprocessing technique must be able to disambiguate amongst the possible analyses of a word, identify the features addressed by the scheme in the chosen analysis and process them as specified by the scheme. In this section we describe eleven different schemes and three techniques. Not all schemes can be created using all techniques. One scheme is a baseline that is created with minimal tokenization prior to applying any of the techniques.

4.1 Preprocessing techniques

The different techniques we chose illustrate three degrees of linguistic knowledge dependence. The first is very light and cheap. The second is more expensive requiring the use of a morphological analyzer. And the third is yet more expensive than the second; it is a disambiguation system that requires an analyzer and a disambiguated training corpus. We are interested in evaluating the contributions of the heavier linguistic resources to SMT.

4.1.1 *REGEX*

This is the baseline technique we use. It is simply greedy regular expression matching to modify strings and/or split off prefix/suffix substrings that look like clitics indicated by specific schemes. REGEX cannot be used with complex schemes requiring additional information beyond string characters. The only schemes creatable using REGEX are D1, D2 and D3 (see Section 4.2).

4.1.2 *BAMA*

The Buckwalter Arabic Morphological Analyzer (Buckwalter 2002) is used to obtain possible word analyses. Using BAMA prevents incorrect greedy REGEX matches. Since BAMA produces multiple analyses, we always select one in a consistent arbitrary manner: first in a sorted list of analyses. Producing a preprocessing scheme involves removing features from the word analysis and regenerating the word without the split off features. The regeneration ensures that the generated form is appropriately normalized. The generation is completed using the off-the-shelf Arabic morphological generation system Aragen (Habash 2004). More details of this tokenization-as-generation approach are available in (Habash 2007).

4.1.3 *MADA*

The Morphological Analysis and Disambiguation for Arabic (MADA) tool is an off-the-shelf resource for Arabic disambiguation (Habash & Rambow 2005).[4] MADA tags words on 10 orthogonal dimensions: part-of-speech (POS), person, number, gender, voice, aspect, determiner proclitic, conjunctive proclitic, particle proclitic, and pronominal enclitic.[5]

These tags are then used to select (disambiguate) among BAMA analyses. Since MADA is a disambiguation system of word morphology, not word sense, it sometimes produces ties for analyses with the same inflectional features but different lexemes. We resolve these ties in a consistent arbitrary manner: first in a sorted list of analyses. The version of MADA used in this chapter was trained on the Penn Arabic Treebank (PATB) part 1 (Maamouri et al. 2004). Habash & Rambow (2005) report disambiguation accuracy over 96% and word-level tokenization accuracy over 99.3%. The specific tokenization scheme they evaluated is the Penn Arabic Treebank scheme (later referred to in Section 4.2 as TB). Specific analysis selection (in case of ties) and preprocessing are done in a manner similar to that discussed in the previous section (Section 4.1).

4.2 Preprocessing schemes

We discuss next the various preprocessing schemes we studied. Table 1 exemplifies the effect of different schemes on the same sentence.

- ST: Simple Tokenization is the baseline preprocessing scheme. It is limited to splitting off punctuations and numbers from words. For example the last

4. The results reported in this paper are based on the MADA system described in (Habash & Rambow 2005). Later versions of MADA have improved over the earlier version (Habash & Rambow 2007; Roth et al. 2008).

5. Arabic has three additional features that are not handled in (Habash & Rambow 2005): case, state, and mood.

non-white-space string in the example sentence in Table 1, "*trkyA.*" is split into two tokens: "*trkyA*" and ".". An example of splitting numbers from words is the case of the conjunction +و *w+* 'and' which can prefix numerals such as: 15و *w15* 'and 15'. This scheme requires no disambiguation. Any diacritics that appear in the input are removed in this scheme. This scheme is used as input to produce the other schemes.

Table 1. Various preprocessing schemes for وسينهى الرئيس جولته بزيارة الى تركيا '*The president will finish his tour with a visit to Turkey*'

Input	wsynhý	Alrŷys	jwlth	bzyArħ	Alý	trkyA.
Gloss	and will finish	the president	tour his	with visit	to	Turkey
Scheme			**Baseline**			
ST	wsynhý	Alrŷys	jwlth	bzyArħ	Alý	trkyA
	Scheme		**Technique:** MADA **or** BAMA			
ON	wsynhy	Alrŷys	jwlth	bzyArħ	Ǎlý	trkyA
D1	w+ synhy	Alrŷys	jwlth	bzyArħ	Ǎlý	trkyA
D2	w+ s+ ynhy	Alrŷys	jwlth	b+ zyArħ	Ǎlý	trkyA
D3	w+ s+ ynhy	Al+ rŷys	jwlħ+P_{3MS}	b+ zyArħ	Ǎlý	trkyA
WA	w+ synhy	Alrŷys	jwlth	bzyArħ	Ǎlý	trkyA
TB	w+ synhy	Alrŷys	jwlħ+P_{3MS}	b+ zyArħ	Ǎlý	trkyA
BW	w+ s+ y+ nhy	Al+ rŷys	jwl+ħ +h	b+ zyAr +ħ	Ǎlý	trkyA
L1	Ânhý$_{V}$	rŷys$_{N}$	jwlħ$_{NN}$	*zyArħ*$_{N}$	Ǎlý$_{P}$	trkyA$_{PN}$
L2	Ânhý$_{VBP}$	rŷys$_{N N}$	jwlħ$_{NN}$	zyArħ$_{N N}$	Ǎlý$_{IN}$	trkyA$_{NNP}$
EN	w+ s+ Ânhŷ$_{VBP}$ + S_{3MS}	Al+ rŷys$_{NN}$	jwlħ$_{NN}$ +P_{3MS}	*b+ zyArħ*$_{NN}$	Ǎlý$_{IN}$	trkyA$_{NNP}$
	Scheme		**Technique:** REGEX			
ON	wsynhy	Alrŷys	jwlth	bzyArh	Aly	trkyA
D1	w+ synhy	Alrŷys	jwlth	bzyArh	Aly	trkyA
D2	w+ s+ ynhy	Alrŷys	jwlth	b+ zyArh	Aly	trkyA
D3	w+ s+ ynh +y	Al+ rŷys	jwlt +h	b+ zyArh	Al+ +y	trkyA
WA	w+ synhy	Alrŷys	jwlth	bzyArh	Aly	trkyA
TB	w+ synh +y	Alrŷys	jwlt +h	b+ zyArh	Al +y	trkyA

– ON: Orthographic Normalization addresses the issue of sub-optimal spelling in Arabic. For the MADA and BAMA disambiguation techniques, the Buckwalter analyzer produces the optimal spelling for analyzed words. We use the undiacritized Buckwalter answer as the orthographically normalized form. For REGEX, we use a simple set of five generic normalization rules. We conflate ي *y* and ى *ý*; ه *h* and ة *ħ*; all Alif variants (ا *A*, أ *Â*, إ *Ǎ*, آ *Ā*); و *w* and ؤ *ŵ*;

and ى *ŷ* and ء *'*. These rules apply unrestricted to all words. Similar rules are commonly used for Arabic in SMT and IR. An example of ON is the spelling of the last letter in the first and fifth words in the example in Table 1 (*wsynhý* and *Alý*, respectively). In the MADA case, only the first word is changed. In the REGEX case, both words are changed.

- D1, D2, and D3: Decliticization (degree 1, 2 and 3) are schemes that split off clitics in the order described in Section 3. D1 splits off the class of conjunction clitics (*w+* and *f+*). D2 is the same as D1 plus splitting off the class of particles (*l+*, *k+*, *b+* and *s+*). Finally D3 splits off what D2 does in addition to the definite article *Al+* and all pronominal enclitics. A pronominal clitic is represented as its feature representation to preserve its uniqueness. For instance, see the third word in the example in Table 1: *jwlħ+*P_{3MS} 'his tour [lit. tour+his]'. This allows distinguishing between the possessive pronoun and object pronoun, which often look similar.
- WA: Decliticizing the conjunction *w+*. This is the simplest tokenization used beyond ON. It is similar to D1, but without including *f+*. This is included to compare to evidence in its support as best preprocessing scheme for very large data (Och 2005; Al-Haj & Lavie 2010).
- TB: Arabic Treebank Tokenization. This is the same tokenization scheme used in the Penn Arabic Treebank (Maamouri et al. 2004). This is similar to D3 but without the splitting off of the definite article *Al+* or the future particle *s+*.[6]
- MR: Morphemes. This scheme breaks up words into stem and affixival morphemes. It is identical to the initial tokenization used by Lee (2004).
- L1 and L2: Lexeme and POS. These reduce a word to its lexeme and a POS. L1 and L2 differ in the set of POS tags they use. L1 uses the simple POS tags advocated by Habash & Rambow (2005) (15 tags); while L2 uses the reduced Penn Arabic Treebank tag set (Maamouri et al. 2004) used by Diab et al. (2004) (24 tags). The latter is modeled after the English Penn POS tag set. For example, Arabic nouns are differentiated for being singular (NN) or Plural/Dual (NNS), but adjectives are not even though, in Arabic, they inflect exactly the same way nouns do.
- EN: English-like. This scheme is intended to minimize differences between Arabic and English. It decliticizes similarly to D3, but uses Lexeme and POS tags instead of the regenerated word. The POS tag set used is the reduced Arabic Treebank tag set (24 tags) (Maamouri et al. 2004; Diab et al. 2004). This set is modeled after the English Penn POS tagset. For example, Arabic

6. In the latest version of the Penn Arabic Treebank, e.g. PATB 3v3.1 (Maamouri et al. 2009), the future particle *s+* is now split unlike earlier versions.

nouns are differentiated for being singular (NN) or Plural/Dual (NNS), but adjectives (JJ) are not even though in Arabic they inflect exactly the same way nouns do. Additionally, the subject inflection is indicated explicitly as a separate token. We do not use any additional information to remove specific features using alignments or syntax unlike, e.g. removing all but one *Al+* in noun phrases (Lee 2004).

4.3 Comparing various schemes

Table 2 compares the different schemes in terms of the number of tokens, number of out-of-vocabulary (OOV) tokens, and perplexity. These statistics are computed over the MT04 set (1353 sentences), which we use in this chapter to report SMT results (Section 5). Perplexity is measured against a language model constructed from the Arabic side of the parallel corpus used in the MT experiments (Section 5). Obviously the more verbose a scheme is, the bigger the number of tokens in the text.

Table 2. Scheme statistics over NIST MT04 set (1353 sentences)

Scheme	Tokens	OOVs	Perplexity
ST	36000	1345	1164
ON	36000	1212	944
D1	38817	1016	582
D2	40934	835	422
D3	52085	575	137
WA	38635	1044	596
TB	42880	662	338
MR	62410	409	69
L1	36000	392	401
L2	36000	432	460
EN	55525	432	103

The ST, ON, L1, and L2 share the same number of tokens because they all modify the word without splitting off any of its morphemes or features. The increase in the number of tokens is in inverse correlation with the number of OOVs and perplexity. The only exceptions are L1 and L2, whose low OOV rate is the result of the reductionist nature of the scheme, which does not preserve morphological information. Finally, the more complex the scheme, the higher the error ratio. For example, Habash & Rambow (2005) report over 99% word accuracy for TB-style tokenization but around 96% accuracy for full morphological tagging, which is necessary for EN and MR schemes. For lexeme selection alone, basic MADA accuracy is around 81%.[7]

5. Experiments

We now describe the system and the data sets we used to conduct our experiments.

5.1 Portage

We use an off-the-shelf phrase-based SMT system, Portage (Sadat et al. 2005). For training, Portage uses IBM word alignment models (models 1 and 2) trained in both directions to extract phrase tables in a manner resembling (Koehn 2004a). Trigram language models are implemented using the SRILM toolkit (Stolcke 2002). Decoding weights are optimized using Och's algorithm (Och 2003) to set weights for the four components of the log-linear model: language model, phrase translation model, distortion model, and word-length feature. The weights are optimized over the BLEU metric (Papineni et al. 2002). The Portage decoder, Canoe, is a dynamic-programming beam search algorithm resembling the algorithm described in (Koehn 2004a).

5.2 Experimental data

All of the training data we use is available from the Linguistic Data Consortium (LDC). We use an Arabic-English parallel corpus of about 5 million words for translation model training data. The parallel text includes Arabic News (LDC2004T17), eTIRR (LDC2004E72), English translation of Arabic Treebank (LDC2005E46), and Ummah (LDC2004T18).

We created the English language model from the English side of the parallel corpus together with 116 million words from the English Gigaword Corpus (LDC2005T12) and 128 million words from the English side of the UN Parallel corpus (LDC2004E13). The SRILM toolkit has a limit on the size of the training corpus. We selected portions of additional corpora using a heuristic that picks documents containing the word "Arab" only. The Language model created using this heuristic had a bigger improvement in BLEU score (more than 1% BLEU-4) than a randomly selected portion of equal size.

English preprocessing simply included down-casing, separating punctuation from words and splitting off "'s". The same preprocessing was used on the English data for all experiments. Only Arabic preprocessing was varied. Decoding weight optimization was done using a set of 200 sentences from the 2003 NIST MT

7. MADA's performance on lexemes is higher in later versions (Habash & Rambow 2007).

evaluation test set MT03. We used two different test sets: (a) the 2004 NIST MT evaluation test set (MT04) and (b) the 2005 NIST MT evaluation test set (MT05). The two sets are chosen because they have a well-known difference: MT04 is a mix of news and other genres (editorials and speeches), whereas MT05 is purely news. We investigate the effects of this difference in Section 5.4. The experiment design and choices of schemes and techniques were done independently of these test sets. All three data sets, MT03, MT04 and MT05, include one Arabic source and four English reference translations. We use the evaluation metric BLEU-4 (Papineni et al. 2002) although we are aware of its caveats (Callison-Burch et al. 2006).

5.3 Experimental results

We conducted all possible combinations of schemes and techniques discussed in Section 4 with different training corpus sizes: 1%, 10%, 50% and 100%. Although Arabic has a lot of parallel resources, most of these resources are in modern standard Arabic (MSA) and within specific genre (news or UN documents). We are interested in looking at limited resource conditions (1% and 10% training) to simulate the situation for Arabic dialects and for impoverished genres. The results of the experiments are summarized in Tables 3 and 4. These results are not English case sensitive. All reported scores must have over 1.1% BLEU-4 difference to be significant at the 95% confidence level for 1% training. For all other training sizes, the difference must be over 1.7% BLEU-4. Error intervals were computed using bootstrap re-sampling (Koehn 2004b).

Table 3. MT04 results with MADA, BAMA and REGEX techniques for different training data sizes. The baseline scheme ST is the same for all techniques

Scheme	MADA				BAMA				REGEX			
	1%	10%	50%	100%	1%	10%	50%	100%	1%	10%	50%	100%
ST	9.42	22.92	31.09	34.59	9.42	22.92	31.09	34.59	9.42	22.92	31.09	34.59
ON	10.71	24.30	32.52	35.91	10.97	24.60	32.62	36.06	10.97	24.14	31.69	35.03
D1	13.11	26.38	33.38	36.06	12.89	26.50	33.67	35.59	11.36	25.47	32.95	34.77
D2	14.19	27.72	35.91	37.10	13.65	27.94	34.58	36.23	11.96	25.53	33.68	35.82
D3	16.51	28.69	34.04	34.33	15.93	28.32	33.73	34.18	13.57	26.11	33.06	34.00
WA	13.12	26.29	34.24	35.97	12.47	27.30	33.57	35.52	11.16	24.95	33.86	34.94
TB	14.13	28.71	35.83	36.76	12.78	27.51	35.63	36.92	12.58	26.18	33.07	34.99
BW	11.61	27.49	32.99	34.43	14.24	27.51	32.20	33.35	n/a	n/a	n/a	n/a
L1	14.63	24.72	31.04	32.23	14.19	26.29	29.65	32.62	n/a	n/a	n/a	n/a
L2	14.87	26.72	31.28	33.00	14.58	26.58	32.59	32.71	n/a	n/a	n/a	n/a
EN	17.45	28.41	33.28	34.51	16.29	27.94	32.66	34.05	n/a	n/a	n/a	n/a

Table 4. MT05 results with MADA, BAMA and REGEX techniques for different training data sizes. The baseline scheme ST is the same for all techniques

Scheme	MADA				BAMA				REGEX			
	1%	10%	50%	100%	1%	10%	50%	100%	1%	10%	50%	100%
ST	11.16	27.72	34.61	37.83	11.16	27.72	34.61	37.83	11.16	27.72	34.61	37.83
ON	12.59	27.43	34.73	37.93	12.64	27.82	34.38	37.62	12.91	28.28	35.42	38.81
D1	14.86	29.75	35.01	37.3	14.50	29.62	35.21	37.06	13.15	29.49	36.42	38.49
D2	16.32	30.21	37.30	38.56	15.50	30.99	35.10	37.75	13.41	29.78	36.22	38.71
D3	17.72	30.95	35.58	36.02	17.28	31.11	35.34	35.29	14.69	28.79	34.17	36.09
WA	15.03	29.45	36.69	37.79	14.57	30.36	35.03	36.56	12.98	28.98	36.28	38.45
TB	15.94	30.96	37.25	37.81	14.40	29.85	36.59	38.34	13.69	29.22	35.83	37.59
BW	12.74	29.55	34.28	35.85	15.68	29.52	33.58	34.33	n/a	n/a	n/a	n/a
L1	16.45	27.67	32.53	33.92	16.47	30.12	32.50	34.97	n/a	n/a	n/a	n/a
L2	16.90	30.51	32.07	34.73	16.44	29.48	34.07	33.92	n/a	n/a	n/a	n/a
EN	18.25	30.42	34.46	36.02	17.56	30.44	34.15	34.79	n/a	n/a	n/a	n/a

5.4 Discussion

Across different schemes, EN performs the best under scarce-resource condition; and D2 performs best under large-resource condition. Across techniques and under scarce-resource conditions, MADA is better than BAMA, which is better than REGEX. Under large-resource conditions, this difference between techniques is statistically insignificant, though it's generally sustained across schemes. The results from the learning curve are consistent with previous published work on using morphological preprocessing for SMT, e.g. Lee (2004): deeper morph analysis helps for small data sets, but the effect is diminished with more data. One interesting observation is that for our best performing system (D2/MADA), the BLEU score for MT04 at 50% training (35.91) was higher than the baseline ST at 100% training data (34.59) (Table 3). This relationship is not consistent across the rest of the experiments. ON improves over the baseline but it is only statistically significant at the 1% level. The results for WA are generally similar to D1. This makes sense since w+ is by far the most common of the two conjunctions D1 splits off. The TB scheme behaves similarly to D2, the best scheme we have. It outperformed D2 in few instances, but the differences were not statistically significant. Given the larger presence of this scheme (as in the Penn Arabic Treebanks), it may be a better choice to use for researchers working on syntactic preprocessing for SMT. L1 and L2 behaved similar to EN across the different training size. However, both were always worse than EN. Neither variant was consistently better than the other.

Table 5. MT04 genre variation for best schemes (BLEU)

	1%		100%	
	News	No News	News	No News
ST	11.9	7.1	40.6	29.1
MADA	**20.4** (EN)	**14.6** (EN)	**41.5** (D2)	**32.6** (D2)
BAMA	19.2 (EN)	13.5 (EN)	40.9 (D2)	31.6 (D2)
REGEX	15.9 (D3)	11.3 (D3)	40.3 (D2)	31.4 (D2)

5.5 Genre variation

The baseline for MT05 is considerably higher than MT04. One explanation is that MT05 is all news genre (same as training data), while MT04 has a mix of genres. To investigate the effect of different schemes and techniques on different genres, we isolated in MT04 those sentences that come from the editorial and speech genres. We performed similar experiments as reported above on this subset of MT04. We found that the effect of the choice of the preprocessing technique+scheme was amplified. For example, MADA+D2 (with 100% training) on non-news improved the system score 12% over the baseline ST (statistically significant) as compared to 2.4% for news only (See Table 5).

5.6 Phrase size

We experimented with larger phrase sizes to investigate any interaction between different schemes and phrase length since some schemes are more verbose than others. There was almost no difference between phrase length of 8 and of 14. We understand this as an indication that a phrase length of 8 is large enough to make phrase length an irrelevant factor for comparing different schemes.

6. Scheme combination

The complementary variation in the behavior of different schemes under different resource size conditions motivated us to investigate system combination. The intuition is that even under large resource conditions, some words will occur very infrequently that the only way to model them is to use a technique that behaves well under poor resource conditions. In the rest of this section, we present an oracle study that validates the potential value of combination. We then describe two scheme-combination techniques: rescoring-only combination (ROC), and decoding-plus-rescoring combination (DRC). All of the experiments use the same training data, test data (MT04) and preprocessing schemes created using the MADA technique since it scored best in our experiments above.

6.1 Oracle experiment

We conducted an oracle study into system combination. We created an oracle combination output by selecting for each input sentence the output with the highest sentence-level BLEU score. We recognize that since the brevity penalty in BLEU is applied globally, this score may not be the highest possible combination score. The oracle combination has a 24% improvement in BLEU score (from 37.1 in best system to 46.0) when combining all eleven schemes described in this chapter. This shows that combining outputs from all schemes has a large potential of improvement over all of the different systems and that the different schemes are complementary in some way.

6.2 Rescoring-only combination

In this "shallow" approach to combination, we rescore all the one-best outputs generated from separate scheme-specific systems and return the top choice. Each scheme-specific system uses its own scheme-specific preprocessing, phrase-tables, and decoding weights. For rescoring, we use the following features:

- The four basic features used by the decoder: trigram language model, phrase translation model, distortion model, and word-length feature.
- IBM model 1 and IBM model 2 probabilities in both directions. We call the union of these two sets of features standard.
- The perplexity of the preprocessed source sentence (PPL) against a source language model as described in Section 4.2.
- The number of out-of-vocabulary words in the preprocessed source sentence (OOV).
- Length of the preprocessed source sentence (SL).
- An encoding of the specific scheme used (SC). We use a one-hot coding approach with 11 separate binary features, each corresponding to a specific scheme.

Optimization of the weights on the rescoring features is carried out using the same max BLEU algorithm and the same development corpus described in Section 5.

Results of different sets of features with the ROC approach are presented in Table 6. Using standard features with all eleven schemes, we obtain a BLEU score of 34.87 – a significant drop from the best scheme system (D2, 37.10). Using different subsets of features or limiting the number of systems to the best four systems (D2,

TB, D1 and WA), we get some improvements. The best results are obtained using all schemes with standard features plus perplexity and scheme coding. The improvements are small; however, they are statistically significant (see Section 6.4).

6.3 Decoding-plus-rescoring combination

This "deep" approach allows the decoder to consult several different phrase tables, each generated using a different preprocessing scheme. This decoding combination stage is followed with a rescoring stage similar to that of ROC. A problem with DRC is that the decoder we use can only cope with one format for the source sentence at a time. Thus, we are forced to designate a particular scheme as privileged when the system is carrying out decoding. The privileged preprocessing scheme will be the one applied to the source sentence. Obviously, words and phrases in the preprocessed source sentence will more frequently match the phrases in the privileged phrase table than in the non-privileged ones. Nevertheless, the decoder may still benefit from having access to all the tables. For each choice of a privileged scheme, optimization of log-linear weights is carried out (with the version of the development set preprocessed in the same privileged scheme).

Table 6. ROC approach results for MT04 (baseline ST = 34.59, best scheme D2 = 37.10)

Combination	All schemes	4 best schemes
standard	34.87	37.12
+PPL+SC	**37.58**	**37.45**
+PPL+SC+OOV	37.40	
+PPL+SC+OOV+SL	37.39	
+PPL+SC+SL	37.15	

The middle column of Table 7 shows the results for 1-best output from the decoder under different choices of the privileged scheme. The best-performing system in this column has as its privileged preprocessing scheme TB. The decoder for this system uses TB to preprocess the source sentence, but has access to a log-linear combination of information from all 11 preprocessing schemes.

The final column of Table 7 shows the results of rescoring the 1-best outputs from the decoding combination stage. The rescoring features used are the same as those used for the ROC experiments. The rescoring stage yielded the best result so far: 38.67 BLEU. Combining the 4 best pre-processing schemes (D2, TB, D1, WA) yielded a lower BLEU score (37.73). These results show that combining phrase tables from different (even low performing) schemes has a positive effect on MT performance.

Table 7. DRC approach results for MT04 (baseline ST = 34.59, best scheme D2 = 37.10)

Combination	Decoding		Rescoring
	Scheme	1-best	Standard+PPL
	D2	37.16	
All schemes	TB	38.24	**38.67**
	D1	37.89	
	WA	36.91	
	ON	36.42	
	ST	34.27	
	EN	30.78	
	MR	34.65	
	D3	34.73	
	L2	32.25	
	L1	30.47	
	D2	37.39	
4 best schemes	TB	37.53	**37.73**
	D1	36.05	
	WA	37.53	

6.4 Significance test

As is shown in Table 8, we use bootstrap re-sampling to compute MT statistical significance as described in (Koehn 2004a). Comparing the 11 individual systems and the two combinations DRC and ROC shows that DRC is significantly better than the other systems – DRC got a max BLEU score in 100% of samples. When excluding DRC from the comparison set, ROC got max BLEU score in 97.7% of samples, while D2 and TB got max BLEU score in 2.2% and 0.1% of samples, respectively. The differences among ROC, D2 and TB are statistically significant.

Table 8. Statistical significance using bootstrap resampling

DRC	ROC	D2	TB	D1	WA	ON
100	0	0	0	0	0	0
	97.7	2.2	0.1	0	0	0
		92.1	7.9	0	0	0
			98.8	0.7	0.3	0.2
				53.8	24.1	22.1
					59.3	40.7

7. Conclusions

We motivated, described and evaluated several preprocessing schemes for Arabic. The choice of a preprocessing scheme is related to the size of available training data. We also presented two techniques for scheme combination. Our results are as follows: (a) for large training data sets, splitting off only conjunctions, prepositions and pre-verbal particles performs best; (b) for small training data sets, following an English-like tokenization and using part-of-speech tags performs best; (c) suitable choice of preprocessing yields an important increase in BLEU score if there is little training data, and/or there is a change in genre between training and test data; (d) sophisticated morphological analysis and disambiguation help significantly in the absence of large data sets; (e) combining systems using different schemes at the target level, the phrase-table level or both improves MT performance.

Acknowledgments

This material is based upon work supported by the Defense Advanced Research Projects Agency (DARPA) under Contract No. HR0011-06-C-0023. Any opinions, findings and conclusions or recommendations expressed in this material are those of the author(s) and do not necessarily reflect the views of the Defense Advanced Research Projects Agency (DARPA). We thank Roland Kuhn, George Forster, Mona Diab, Owen Rambow, and Martin Jansche for helpful discussions.

References

Al-Haj, H., and A. Lavie. 2010. The impact of Arabic morphological segmentation on broad coverage English-to-Arabic statistical machine translation. In *Proceedings of the Conference of the Association for Machine Translation in the Americas* (AMTA).

Badr, I., R. Zbib, and J. Glass. 2008. Segmentation for English-to-Arabic statistical machine translation. In *Proceedings of ACL-08: HLT, Short Papers*, 153–156 Columbus OH.

Bangalore, S., G. Bordel, and G. Riccardi. 2001. Computing consensus translation from multiple machine translation systems. In *Proceedings of IEEE Automatic Speech Recognition and Understanding Workshop.*

Bender, O., E. Matusov, S. Hahn, S.S. Hasan, S. Khadivi, and H. Ney. 2007. The RWTH Arabic-to-English spoken language translation system. In *Proceedings of the IEEE Automatic Speech Recognition and Understanding Workshop* (ASRU 2007), 396–401.

Berger, A., P. Brown, S. Pietra, V. Pietra, J. Gillett, J. Lafferty, R. Mercer, H. Printz, and L. Ures. 1994. The Candide system for machine translation. In *Proceedings of the ARPA Conference on Human Language Technology.*

Bertoldi, N., A. Bisazza, M. Cettolo, G. Sanchis-Trilles, and M. Federico. 2009. FBK @ IWSLT 2009. In: IWSLT 2009: International Workshop on Spoken Language Translation.

Buckwalter, T. 2002. Buckwalter Arabic Morphological Analyzer Version 1.0. Linguistic Data Consortium, University of Pennsylvania. LDC Catalog No.: LDC2002L49.

Callison-Burch, C., M. Osborne, and P. Koehn. 2006. Re-evaluating the role of BLEU in machine translation research. In Proceedings of the 11th conference of the European Chapter of the Association for Computational Linguistics (EACL'06), 249–256.

de Gispert, A. 2006. Introducing Linguistic Knowledge into Statistical Machine Translation. Ph.D dissertation, Universitat Politècnica de Catalunya.

de Gispert, A., S. Virpioja, M. Kurimo, and W. Byrne. 2009. Minimum Bayes risk combination of translation hypotheses from alternative morphological decompositions. In *Proceedings of the North American Chapter of the Association for Computational Linguistics, Short Papers*. Boulder CO.

Diab, M., K. Hacioglu, and D. Jurafsky. 2004. Automatic tagging of Arabic text: From raw text to base phrase chunks. In Proceedings of the North American Chapter of the Association for Computational Linguistics/Human Language Technologies Conference (HLT-NAACL04), 149–152.

Diehl, F., M. J. F. Gales, M. Tomalin, and P. C. Woodland. 2009. Morphological analysis and decomposition for Arabic speech-to-text systems. In *Proceedings of InterSpeech*.

El Isbihani, A., S. Khadivi, O. Bender, and H. Ney. 2006. Morpho-syntactic Arabic preprocessing for Arabic to English statistical machine translation. In *Proceedings of the Workshop on Statistical Machine Translation*. New York NY.

El Kholy, A., and N. Habash. 2010a. Orthographic and morphological processing for English-Arabic statistical machine translation. In *Proceedings of Traitement Automatique des Langues Naturelles* (TALN-10). Montréal, Canada.

El Kholy, A., and N. Habash. 2010b. Techniques for Arabic morphological detokenization and orthographic denormalization. In *Workshop on Language Resources and Human Language Technology for Semitic Languages in the Language Resources and Evaluation Conference* (LREC).

Elming, J., and N. Habash. 2007. Combination of statistical word alignments based on multiple preprocessing schemes. In *Proceedings of the North American Chapter of the Association for Computational Linguistics, Short Papers*. Rochester NY.

Frederking, R., and S. Nirenburg. 1994. Three heads are better than one. In *Proceedings of the Fourth Conference on Applied Natural Language Processing* (ANLP-94).

Goldwater, S., and D. McClosky. 2005. Improving statistical MT through morphological analysis. In *Proceedings of the Conference on Empirical Methods in Natural Language Processing* (EMNLP), 676–683.

Habash, N. 2004. Large scale lexeme based Arabic morphological generation. In *Proceedings of Traitement Automatique des Langues Naturelles* (TALN-04). 271–276. Fez, Morocco.

Habash, N. 2007. Arabic morphological representations for machine translation. In *Arabic Computational Morphology: Knowledge-based and Empirical Methods*, Antal van den Bosch, Abdelhadi Soudi & Güther Neumann (eds). Dordrecht: Springer.

Habash, N. 2010. *Introduction to Arabic Natural Language Processing*. San Rafael CA: Morgan & Claypool.

Habash, N., and O. Rambow. 2005. Arabic tokenization, part-of-speech tagging and morphological disambiguation in one fell swoop. In *Proceedings of the Association for Computational Linguistics* (ACL'05). Ann Arbor MI.

Habash, N. and O. Rambow. 2007. Arabic diacritization through full morphological tagging. In *Proceedings of the North American Chapter of the Association for Computational Linguistics; Companion Volume, Short Papers*. Rochester NY.

Habash, N., and F. Sadat. 2006. Arabic preprocessing schemes for statistical machine translation. In *Proceedings of the Human Language Technology Conference of the NAACL, Companion Volume: Short Papers*. New York NY.

Habash, N., A. Soudi, and T. Buckwalter. 2007. On Arabic transliteration. In *Arabic Computational Morphology: Knowledge-based and Empirical Methods*, Antal van den Bosch, Abdelhadi Soudi & Günther Neumann (eds). Dordrecht: Springer.

Jayaraman, S., and A. Lavie. 2005. Multi-engine machine translation guided by explicit word matching. In *Proceedings of the 10th Annual Conference of the European Association for Machine Translation* (EAMT 2005).

Koehn, P. 2004a. Pharaoh: A beam search decoder for phrase-based statistical machine translation models. In *Proceedings of the Association for Machine Translation in the Americas*.

Koehn, P. 2004b. Statistical significance tests for machine translation evaluation. In *Proceedings of the Empirical Methods in Natural Language Processing Conference* (EMNLP'04).

Larkey, L. S., L. Ballesteros, and M. E. Connell. 2007. Light stemming for Arabic information retrieval. In *Arabic Computational Morphology: Knowledge-based and Empirical Methods*. Dordrecht: Springer.

Lee, Y.-S. 2004. Morphological analysis for statistical machine translation. In *Proceedings of the North American Chapter of the Association for Computational Linguistics/Human Language Technologies Conference* (HLT-NAACL04).

Lee, Y-S. 2005. IBM statistical machine translation for spoken languages. In *Proceedings of the International Workshop on Spoken Language Translation* (IWSLT 2005).

Maamouri, M., A. Bies, T. Buckwalter, and W. Mekki. 2004. The Penn Arabic Treebank: Building a large-scale annotated Arabic corpus.

Maamouri, M., A. Bies, and S. Kulick. 2009. Creating a methodology for large-scale correction of treebank annotation: The case of the Arabic treebank. In *Proceedings of MEDAR International Conference on Arabic Language Resources and Tools.*

Matusov, E., N. Ueffing, and H. Ney. 2006. Computing consensus translation from multiple machine translation systems using enhanced hypotheses alignment. In *Proceedings of EACL*.

Nießen, S., and H. Ney. 2004. Statistical machine translation with scarce resources using morpho-syntactic information. *Computational Linguistics* 30 (2).

Nomoto, T. 2004. Multi-engine machine translation with voted language model. In *Proceedings of the 42nd Meeting of the Association for Computational Linguistics (ACL'04), Main Volume*, 494–501

Och, F. J. 2003. Minimum error rate training for statistical machine translation. In *Proceedings of the 41st Annual Conference of the Association for Computational Linguistics*, 160–167.

Och, F. J. 2005. Google system description for the 2005 NIST MT evaluation. Presented at *MT Eval Workshop*.

Papineni, K., S. Roukos, T. Ward, and W.-J. Zhu. 2002. BLEU: A method for automatic evaluation of machine translation. In *Proceedings of the Association for Computational Linguistics*.

Paul, M., T. Doi, Y. Hwang, K. Imamura, H. Okuma, and E. Sumita. 2005. Nobody is perfect: ATR's hybrid approach to spoken language translation. In *Proceedings of the International Workshop on Spoken Language Translation* (IWSLT 2005).

Popovic, M., and H. Ney. 2004. Towards the use of word stems and suffixes for statistical machine translation. In *Proceedings of the 4th International Conference on Language Resources and Evaluation* (LREC), 1585–1588.

Riesa, J., and D. Yarowsky. 2006. Minimally supervised morphological segmentation with applications to machine translation. In *Proceedings of the Conference of the Association for Machine Translation in the Americas* (AMTA06).

Roth, R., O. Rambow, N. Habash, M. Diab, and C. Rudin. 2008. Arabic morphological tagging, diacritization, and lemmatization using lexeme models and feature ranking. In *Proceedings of ACL-08: HLT, Short Papers*. Columbus OH.

Sadat, F., and N. Habash. 2006. Combination of Arabic preprocessing schemes for statistical machine translation. In *Proceedings of the Conference on Computational Linguistics and 44th Annual Meeting of the Association for Computational Linguistics*. Sydney, Australia.

Sadat, F., H. Johnson, A. Agbago, G. Foster, R. Kuhn, J. Martin, and A. Tikuisis. 2005. Portage: A phrase-based machine translation system. In *Proceedings of the ACL 2005 Workshop on Building and Using Parallel Texts*.

Stolcke, A. 2002. SRILM an extensible language modeling toolkit. In *Proceedings of the International Conference on Spoken Language Processing* (ICSLP), Vol. 2.

Čmejrek, M., J. Curín, J. Havelka, J. Hajič, and V. Kubon. 2004. Prague Czech-English dependency treebank: Syntactically annotated resources for machine translation". In *Proceedings of the Conference on Language Resources and Evaluation* (LREC).

Yang, M., J. Zheng, and A. Kathol. 2007. A semi-supervised learning approach for morpheme segmentation for an Arabic dialect. In *Proceedings of Interspeech*.

Zitouni, I, J. Sorensen, X. Luo, and R. Florian. 2005. The impact of morphological stemming on Arabic mention detection and coreference resolution. In *Proceedings of the ACL Workshop on Computational Approaches to Semitic Languages*.

Zollmann, A., A. Venugopal, and S. Vogel. 2006. Bridging the inflection morphology gap for Arabic statistical machine translation. In *Proceedings of the Human Language Technology Conference of the NAACL, Companion Volume: Short Papers*. New York NY.

Preprocessing for English-to-Arabic Statistical Machine Translation

Rabih Zbib & Ibrahim Badr
Raytheon BBN Technologies, Cambridge MA, USA / Massachusetts Institute of Technology, Cambridge MA, USA

Most research in Arabic Statistical Machine Translation (SMT) has focused on translating from Arabic into English and other languages. Translation to Arabic has drawn very little attention so far, despite being an important, as well as technically challenging task. This chapter describes the application of two preprocessing techniques to English-to-Arabic SMT: Morphological Segmentation and Syntactic Reordering. It shows how these techniques can be adapted to apply to translation into Arabic, providing significant improvements to a phrase-based system.

1. Introduction

Previous research in the area of Arabic machine translation has almost exclusively concentrated on issues arising from the translation of Arabic to English. Very little work has been done on SMT from English or other languages into Arabic. However, developing automatic translation technologies into Arabic is as important, since it opens access for Arabic speakers to the vast amounts of knowledge available in English and other world languages. Machine translation into Arabic presents new technical challenges as well. The characteristic challenge for machine translation from Arabic to English is to deal with the large size of the source vocabulary relative to English, which is due to the morphological complexity of Arabic. When translating into Arabic on the other hand, morphologically complex words have to be generated on the target side, and grammatical agreement constraints have to be respected.

Preprocessing techniques can be used effectively in SMT to transform one or both languages before translation rules are applied. Arbitrary transformations can be performed as long as they are done consistently for both training and decoding. When they are done on the target side, a post-process is required to transform the output to the regular form of the language. In this chapter, we describe how preprocessing techniques that have been used for Arabic-to-English SMT can be adapted for English-to-Arabic SMT. The first method is morphological segmentation of the Arabic target, where we describe techniques for recombining the segmented Arabic. The second method is to apply predefined reorder rules on the parse tree of the English source to result in a structure that is closer to the Arabic syntax. We show improvements from both methods when applied to a phrase-based English-to-Arabic SMT system. This chapter expands on the work in Badr et al. (2008) and Badr et al. (2009).

2. Morphological preprocessing for English-to-Arabic SMT

2.1 Morphological segmentation of Arabic

Separating the stems and affixed morphemes of Arabic words before the text is aligned to English reduces the size of the vocabulary on the Arabic side, and also the out-of-vocabulary (OOV) rate. The decreased sparseness of training data allows for a more robust estimation of the translation model parameters. Also, segmented Arabic can be better aligned to the English side since fewer many-to-one alignments are required as a result. Morphological segmentation has been successfully applied to machine translation from Arabic to English and other languages (Lee 2004; Habash & Sadat 2006). Chapter 5 presents a detailed study of different morphological segmentations schemes for Arabic, and their effect on Arabic-English machine translation. As Chapter 5 explains, the separation of affixes cannot be done through simple pattern matching, though. Determining whether a given string is an affix or part of the stem itself requires morphological analysis that draws on morphological, lexical and contextual knowledge to determine the morphemes that constitute a word in context. In this case, we use the statistical morphological analyzer MADA (Habash & Rambow 2005), which is also used in Chapter 5, to perform morphological analysis on the Arabic side of the training data.

2.2 Recombination of segmented Arabic

In the proposed method the decoder is trained on segmented Arabic, and will therefore produce segmented Arabic translations, which need to be recombined in order to produce the final Arabic output. Recombination is not a trivial step for a number of reasons:

1. **Morpho-phonological Rules**: When morphemes combine, they sometimes undergo phonological modification as a result, which can be reflected in the orthography. For example, the feminine marker '*ħ*' at the end of a word

changes to '*t*' when a suffix is attached to the word. So *syArħ +y* recombines to *syArty* ('my car'). The morphological splitter MADA restores the proper form of the stem upon splitting. It is important for the segmented stem to be represented in their proper form for a couple of reasons:

a. If the proper form of the stem is not restored upon splitting, the data will contain an unnecessarily large vocabulary size. If *syArty* is split to *syArt +y*, then the data would contain two forms of the stem: *syArħ* and *syArt*, which unnecessarily increases the sparseness of the training.
b. The decoder will produce stems in their normal form next to split morphemes, and the post-processing should be able to recombine those properly. So even if *syArt +y* is not normalized, the decoder might still produce *syAr ħ +y*, which the post-processor should be able to combine into the proper form *syArty.*

2. **Letter Ambiguity**: Data sources are inconsistent in spelling. For example, the character '*y*' is often misspelled as '*ý*' *(Âlif mqSwrħ)*, at the end of the word. We normalize '*ý*' to '*y*' to make the data more consistent. The recombination procedure needs to be able to decide whether a final '*y*' was originally a '*ý*'. For example, *mdý +h* recombines to *mdAh* ('its extent'), since the final '*y*' is actually a '*ý*' that in turn is transformed into a 'A' when attached. On the other hand, *fy +h* recombines to *fyh* ('in it').
3. **Word Ambiguity**: In some cases, a morpheme tuple *(prefix(es)+stem+suffix)* can be recombined into two different valid forms. One example is the optional insertion of '*n*' (called *nwn AlwqAyħ, 'protective n'* in classical grammar), between the stem and the first person object pronoun. So the segmented word *lkn +y 'but I am'* can recombine to one of the two forms: *lknny* and *lkny*, both valid.

Given the above reasons, a simple concatenation of the split morphemes would not produce correct Arabic text. We propose a number of recombination schemes to deal with these issues:

1. **Recombination Scheme R.** Recombination rules are defined manually. To resolve word ambiguity, the grammatical form that appears most frequently in the training data is picked. To resolve letter ambiguity, we use a unigram language model trained on data for which character normalization has not been performed, and choose the most frequent form.
2. **Recombination Scheme T.** This scheme uses a table derived from the training set that maps the segmented form of the word to its original form. If a segmented word has more than one original form, one of them is picked at random. The table is useful in recombining words that are split erroneously.

For example *qrDay*, a proper noun, is incorrectly segmented to *qrDAn +y*, so recombining it without the table becomes impossible.

3. **Recombination Scheme T+R.** Attempts to recombine a segmented word using scheme T, and defaults to scheme **R** if that fails.

2.3 Experimental setup

We run machine translation experiments on data from two domains: Arabic newswire from LDC corpora, and ISWL – spoken dialog from the travel domain. For the news domain, we test on 2000 randomly chosen sentences, and vary the size of training between 600K, 1.6M and 3M words to measure the effect of the training corpus size on the improvement obtained from morphological segmentation. 20 million words from the LDC Arabic Gigaword are used for language model training. The average number of English words per sentence is 33, compared to 25 Arabic words before segmentation and 36 words after segmentation. We use the IWSLT 2007 Arabic-English corpus (Fordyce 2007) for the spoken domain. The corpus consists of 200,000 words for training, 500 sentences for tuning and 500 sentences for testing. The Arabic side of the parallel data was used for language modeling. The average sentence length is 9 words for English, 8 for Arabic and 10 for segmented Arabic.

GIZA++ (Och & Ney 2000) was used for alignments, and decoding was done using MOSES (Koehn et al. 2007). The parameter tuning uses Minimum Error Rate Training (MERT) (Och 2003) to optimize system weights over BLEU. Tuning is performed on the segmented Arabic.

Table 1. Recombination results. Percentage of sentences with mis-combined words

	Baseline	R	T	T+R
Training	43.6%	4.04%	N/A	N/A
Tuning	36.8%	4.65%	22.1%	1.9%

2.4 Experimental results

We first test the effectiveness of the different recombination methods on the test sets. The scores in **Table 1.** show the percentage of sentences in the corresponding data set that contain at least one recombination error. The baseline setting corresponds to the naïve approach of directly gluing the affixes to the stem. The results show that the mapping table is more reliable than the rules, presumably because it covers certain special cases that the rules might transform erroneously. Using rules as a back-off method, however, provides additional improvement. The scheme **T+R** is therefore used in the subsequent translation experiments.

Translation scores for newswire data are shown in Table 2, using both segmentation schemes **S1** (affixes are kept separate) and **S2** (split word into at most three parts: prefix+ stem +suffix), as well as different training corpus sizes. As expected, lower training data size results in lower BLEU scores. More interestingly, the gain obtained from morphological segmentation is larger when the size of the training corpus is smaller. This is consistent with the results that Habash and Sadat present in Chapter 5 on morphological segmentation for Arabic-English machine translation.

The reason for the larger gain is that as the size of the training corpus increases, the out-of-vocabulary rate of the non-segmented corpus decreases, and the corresponding translation models become less sparse, hence reducing the benefit obtained from the segmented data. The gain obtained from segmentation on the ISWL data results (Table 3) is larger compared to the newswire data, also due to the smaller amount of training data.

Table 2. BLEU scores for news data with 1 reference

	3 mil.	1.6 mil.	0.6 mil.
Baseline	26.44	20.51	17.93
S1	26.81 (+0.37)	21.93 (+1.42)	20.87 (+2.90)
S2	26.86 (+0.42)	21.99 (+1.48)	20.44 (+2.51)

Table 3. BLEU scores for IWSLT data with 1 reference

	No Tuning	With Tuning
Baseline	26.39	24.67
S1	29.07 (+2.68)	29.82 (+5.15)
S2	29.11 (+2.72)	30.10 (+5.43)

3. Syntactic preprocessing for English-to-Arabic SMT

The previous section described work on the use of morphological preprocessing for English-to-Arabic SMT. This section presents another preprocessing technique, namely syntactic reordering of the English source in order to better match the phrase structure of the Arabic sentence.

Sentence structure, which corresponds to rules of the language grammar that allow constituents to be combined in specific ways, is one of the aspects in which languages can differ considerably. Syntax-based SMT attempts to model these differences directly by using tree-to-tree models. For string-based models though, these differences are manifested as differences in the word order of the corresponding serialized sentences. Local structural relationships (i.e. with respect to the tree structure of the sentence) can thus appear as long distance relationships in the serialized sentence. For this reason, string models such as phrase-based SMT systems have an inherent limitation in dealing with such long distance linguistic phenomena, since they rely on word alignments that are mostly local. Automatically learned reordering models (called distortion models) that can be conditioned on lexical items from both the source and target sides are usually used with string-based SMT models, such as phrase-based SMT, providing limited reordering capability to string-based models. But the reorderings in this case are still applied to the sentence string, rather than to a representation of the deep structure of the sentence. One approach that attempts to deal with long distance reordering, while still using string-based models is to reorder the source side to better match the word order of the target language using predefined rules. This is done as a preprocessing step prior to both training and decoding. The reordering rules are applied to the parse trees of the source sentences, thus indirectly incorporating information on the structure of the source language into the translation process. Despite the added complexity of parsing the data, this technique has been shown to improve on phrase-based SMT, especially when the source language can be parsed reliably.

This section describes the application of a similar approach to English-to-Arabic SMT. A set of syntactic reordering rules are applied on the English side to better align it to the Arabic target. The reordering rules exploit systematic differences in the sentence structures of English and Arabic. They specifically address two syntactic constructs. The first is the Subject-Verb order in independent sentences, where the preferred order in written Arabic is Verb-Subject. The second is the structure of the noun phrase, where many differences between the two languages exit, among them the order of the adjectives, compound nouns, possessive constructs, as well as the way in which definiteness is marked. These transformations are applied to the parse trees of the English source. It has been observed previously, for instance in Habash (2007), that the improvement in translation quality that can be obtained from syntactic reordering depends heavily on the quality of the sentence parses. Since the source language in our case is English, the parses are more reliable, and therefore, the reorderings that are applying based on the parse are more frequently correct. English parsers perform better than parsers of other languages since they have been in development for longer, and state-of-the-art advancements in statistical parsing techniques are usually applied to English first.

3.1 Related work

Habash (2007) uses syntactic reordering rules for Arabic-to-English SMT, where the rules are automatically learned using word alignments. After the sentence pairs are aligned, the Arabic side is parsed to extract the reordering rules. No significant improvement is observed with reordering when compared to the baseline, which uses a non-lexicalized distance reordering model. The author attributes the lack of improvement to the poor quality of the Arabic parses. Syntactic reordering has also been applied to German-to-English and Chinese-to-English SMT (Collins et al. 2005; Wang et al. 2007). Both parse the source side sentences, and then reorder the sentence based on predefined, linguistically motivated rules. Significant translation improvements are reported for both language pairs. Popovic and Ney (2006) use similar methods to reorder German by looking at POS tags of the German source for German-to-English and German-to-Spanish translation. They show significant improvements on test set sentences that do get reordered as well as those that don't. The latter is attributed to the improvement in the extracted phrases. Xia and McCord (2004) also use reordering rules to improve the translation, but with a notable difference: the reordering rules are automatically learned from the alignment of parse trees for both the source and target sentences. The use of automatically-learned rules has the advantage of being readily applicable to different language pairs, since there is no need to define language-specific rules for each source language or language pair. The use of deterministic, predefined rules, however, has the advantage of being linguistically motivated, since structural differences between the two languages are addressed explicitly. Moreover, the implementation of predefined transfer rules based on source-side parses is relatively easy and cheap to do in different language pairs.

3.2 Reordering rules

We next describe the syntax-based rules we used to reorder the English side to better match the syntax of the Arabic target. These rules are applied to the English parse tree at the sentence level or the noun phrase level.

Verb Phrase Rules. The structure of the main sentence in Arabic is Verb-Subject-Object (VSO), as Example 1 shows. The order Subject-Verb-Object is also possible, but less frequent. When the direct object of the verb is a personal pronoun, the pronoun is attached to the verb. So a post-verbal subject has to follow the object pronoun as well (see Example 1c).

(1) a. *Akl* *Alwld* *AltfAHħ*
ate-3SM the-boy the-apple
'the boy ate the apple'

b. *Alwld* *Akl* *AltfAHħ*
the-boy ate-3SM the-apple
'the boy ate the apple'

c. *Akl* *+hA* *AlAwlAd*
ate-3SM it the-boys
'the boys ate it'

In a dependent clause, the order must be SVO, as illustrated by the ungrammaticality of 2b.

(2) a. *qAl* *An* *Alwld* *Akl* *AltfAHħ*
said-3SM that the-boy ate the-apple
'he said that the boy ate the apple'

b. **qAl* *An* *Akl* *Alwld* *AltfAHħ*
said-3SM that ate the-boy the-apple

Another pertinent syntactic property is that the negation particle has to always precede the verb. We define a reordering rule that transfers the English parse tree from SVO order to VSO based on these differences. A check is also performed to make sure that the verb is not in a relative clause. In the following example of a mapped sentence, the main verb *stated* is reordered, while the subordinate clause verb *were wounded* is not:

Example:
Original: *the health minister stated that 11 police officers were wounded in clashes with the demonstrators*
Reordered: *stated the health minister that 11 police officers were wounded in clashes with the demonstrators*

If the verb is negated, then the negation particle is moved together with the verb.

Example:
Original: *click here if associated images do not appear in your mail*
Reordered: *click here if do not appear associated images in your mail*

Finally, if the object of the sentence is a pronoun, then it is moved with the verb to reflect the $VO_{pron}S$ structure mentioned above.

Noun Phrase Rules. The structure of noun phrases in Arabic also differs from that of English in a number of ways. The adjective follows the noun it modifies rather than preceding it. Arabic also uses a special construct called *iDafaħ* to express the possessives, compound nouns and the equivalent of the *of*-relationship in English. So the English constructs N_1*'s* N_2 and N_2 *of* N_1 both correspond to the Arabic N_2 N_1. These phenomena are all shown in Example 3.

(3) *mftAH bAb Albyt Alkbyr*
key door the-house the-big
'the key to the door of the big house'

The differences in the structure of the noun phrase between the two languages are handled by the reordering rules as follows: The order of all nouns, adjectives and adverbs in the noun phrase is inverted. This addresses the difference in noun/adjective order, as well as the *iDafah* construct. The following example shows the reordering of a noun phrase:

Example:
Original: *the blank computer screen*
Reordered: *screen computer the blank*

Prepositional Phrase Rules. This rule is motivated by the correspondence between the *of*-construct in English and the *iDafah* construct in Arabic. All prepositional phrases of the form N_1 *of* N_2 ... *of* N_n are transformed to N_1 N_2 ... *of* N_n. If the prepositional phrase is definite, all definite articles are removed, and a definite article is added to N_n, the last noun in the chain:

Example:
Original: *the general chief of staff of the armed forces*
Reordered: *general chief staff the armed forces*

All adjectives in the top noun phrase are also moved to the end of the construct, since adjectives follow their modifiers as mentioned above.

3.3 Experimental setup

We next describe the setup and data used for the syntactic reordering experiments. The English source is first tokenized and tagged using the Stanford Log-linear Part-of-Speech Tagger (Toutanova 2003), then parsed using the Collins parser (Collins 1997). Person, location and organization names are tagged using the Stanford Named Entity Recognizer (Finkel et al. 2005). On the Arabic side, the data is normalized by changing the final 'ý' to 'y', and changing the various forms of *Alif hamzah* to *Alif*, since these characters are written inconsistently in different Arabic sources. The data is then segmented using MADA, in the same way described above. Also as with the previous section, the English source

Table 4. BLEU scores for syntactic reordering of newswire data

Scheme	RandT		MT 05	
	Seg.	No Seg.	Seg.	No Seg.
Baseline	21.6	21.3	23.88	23.44
VP	21.9	21.5	23.98	23.58
NP	21.9	21.8	–	–
NP+PP	21.8	21.5	23.72	23.68
NP+PP+VP	22.2	21.8	23.74	23.16

is aligned to the reordered Arabic target using the standard MOSES configuration of GIZA++ and decoding is done using MOSES. The setup also uses a bidirectional reordering model conditioned on both the source and target sides, with a distortion limit of 6. Tuning uses MERT training as well to optimize the BLEU score.

Table 5. BLEU scores for syntactic reordering of NIST MT05 set based on sentence length

	Baseline	VP	NP+PP	NP+PP+VP
Short	22.57	22.95	22.71	22.84
Long	25.22	25.05	24.76	24.62

Data Corpora. Experiments were done on data in two domains: newswire text and spoken dialog from the travel domain. Sentences in the travel domain are much shorter than in the news domain, which simplifies the alignment as well as reordering during decoding. Also, since the travel domain contains spoken Arabic, it is more biased towards the Subject-Verb-Object sentence order than the Verb-Subject-Object order, which is more common in the news domain. Since most of the data used was originally intended for Arabic-to-English translation, the test and tuning sets have only one reference, resulting in lower than typical BLEU scores. The news training data is constructed from several LDC corpora. A test set is constructed randomly by picking 2000 sentences from the training data, and the tuning set consists of another 2000 randomly picked sentences. The final training set consists of 3 million words (counted on the English side). The system was also tested on the NIST MT 05 test set, while the NIST MT 03 and 04 test sets were used for tuning. For the language model, we use 35 million words from the LDC Arabic Gigaword corpus, plus the 3 million words consisting of the

Arabic side of the parallel data. The average sentence length is 33 for English, 25 for non-segmented Arabic and 36 for segmented Arabic. For the spoken dialog domain, the BTEC 2007 Arabic-English corpus is used. The training set consists of 200K words, the test set has 500 sentences, and the tuning set has 500 sentences. The language model consists of the Arabic side of the training data. Because of the significantly smaller data size, a trigram LM is used for the baseline, and a 4-gram LM is used for segmented Arabic. In this case, the average sentence length is 9 for English, 8 for Arabic, and 10 for segmented Arabic.

3.4 Results

We next describe and discuss the results for the syntactic reordering experiments. Table 4 shows the BLEU scores for syntactic reordering experiments on the randomly selected (RandT) and the NIST MT05 newswire test sets. Each row shows the score resulting from the application of a different combination of rules. Scores for both morphologically segmented and non-segmented Arabic are shown. The gain from reordering rules is comparable in both cases, showing that the improvement from the two preprocessing techniques is additive. As mentioned earlier, the quality of the parsing has a large effect on the effectiveness of reordering. Parse quality is also correlated with the length of the sentence, since shorter sentences are easier to parse. We show the effect of sentence length on the improvement from reordering in **Table 5**, where the NIST MT05 test set is divided into two subset of short (<40 words) and long (≥40 words) sentences. The results show a varying but consistent gain from the reordering of the short sentences, but not the long ones. This discrepancy further shows the importance of parsing quality for the reordering technique.

Table 6. BLEU scores for syntactic reordering of the Spoken Language Domain

	Baseline	VP	NP	NP+PP
Seg.	29.06	26.92	27.94	28.59
No Seg.	25.40	23.49	26.83	26.42

Finally, results for the BTEC corpus are shown in Table 6. Notice that the relative gain from the application of the reordering rules is significantly higher for this test set than for newswire data, since the sentences are shorter and simpler, and can therefore be parsed more reliably. It is also worth noting that the lack of gain when the verb phrase is reordered is because the preferred sentence order for spoken Arabic is Subject-Verb-Object rather than the Verb-Subject-Object.

4. Summary

Statistical machine translation into Arabic has attracted little attention compared to translation from Arabic. Translating into Arabic, however, is an important, as well as technically challenging problem. There have been new publications on English-to-Arabic machine translation (Sarikaya & Deng 2007; Elming & Habash 2009; El Kholy & Habash 2010). In this chapter, we showed how preprocessing techniques can be used for English-to-Arabic translation in order to narrow the gap between the morphology and the syntax of Arabic and English.

Much work is still needed in this promising area of research, building on work that has been done so far, as well as on machine translating to other morphologically complex languages such as Czech, Russian and Turkish.

References

Badr I., R. Zbib, and J. Glass. 2008. Segmentation for English-to-Arabic statistical machine translation. In *Proceedings of ACL-HLT.*

Badr I., R. Zbib, and J. Glass. 2009. Syntactic phrase reordering for English-to-Arabic statistical machine translation. In *Proceedings of the EACL.*

Collins M. 1997. Three generative, lexicalized models for statistical parsing. In *Proceedings of the ACL.*

Collins M., P. Koehn, and I. Kucerova. 2005. Clause restructuring for statistical machine translation. In *Proceedings of the ACL.*

El Kholy, A., and N. Habash. 2010. Orthographic and morphological processing for English-Arabic statistical machine translation. In *Proceedings of TALN 2010.*

Elming, J., and N. Habash. 2009. Syntactic reordering for English-Arabic phrase-based machine translation. In *Proceedings of the EACL.*

Finkel, J. R., T. Grenager, and C. Manning. 2005. Incorporating non-local information into information extraction systems by Gibbs sampling. In *Proceedings of the ACL.*

Fordyce, C. S. 2007. Overview of the 2007 IWSLT evaluation campaign. In *Proceedings of IWSLT 2007.*

Habash, N., and O. Rambow. 2005. Arabic tokenization, part-of-speech tagging and morphological disambiguation in one fell swoop. In *Proceedings of the ACL.*

Habash, N., and F. Sadat. 2006. Arabic preprocessing schemes for statistical machine translation. In *Proceedings of the Human Language Technology Conference.*

Habash, N. 2007. Syntactic preprocessing for statistical machine translation. In *Proceedings. of the Machine Translation Summit.*

Koehn, P., and H. Hoang. 2007. Factored translation models. In *Proceeding of EMNLP/CNLL.*

Lee, Y.-S. 2004. Morphological analysis for statistical machine translation. In *Proceedings of EMNLP.*

Och, F., and H. Ney. 2000. Improved statistical alignment models. In *Proceedings of the ACL.*

Och, F. 2003. Minimum error rate training in statistical machine translation. In *Proceedings of the ACL.*

Popovic, M., and H. Ney. 2006. POS-based word reordering for statistical machine translation. In *Proceedings of NAACL LREC.*

Sarikaya, R., and Y. Deng. 2007. Joint morphological-lexical language modeling for machine translation. In *Proceedings of NAACL-HLT.*

Wang, C., M. Collins, and P. Koehn. 2007. Chinese syntactic reordering for statistical machine translation. In *Proceedings of EMNLP.*

Xia, F., and M. McCord. 2004. Improving a statistical MT system with automatically learned rewrite patterns. In *Proceedings of COLING.*

Lexical syntax for Arabic SMT

Hany Hassan
Microsoft Research, United States

The current approaches of Phrase-based Statistical Machine Translation lacks the capabilities of producing grammatical translations and handling long-range reordering. In this chapter, we present our work for extending Phrase-based SMT with lexical syntactic descriptions that localize global syntactic information on the word without introducing syntactic redundant ambiguity. We present a novel model of Phrase-based SMT which integrates linguistic lexical descriptions supertags into the target language model and the target side of the translation model. Moreover, we introduce a novel Incremental Dependency-based Syntactic Language Model (IDLM) based on wide-coverage CCG incremental parsing which we integrate into a direct translation SMT system. Our proposed approach is the first to integrate full dependency parsing in SMT systems with a very attractive computational cost since it deploys the linear decoders widely used in Phrase-based SMT systems. The experimental results show a good improvement over top-ranked state-of-the-art systems.

1. Introduction

Statistical Machine Translation (SMT) is by far the most dominant paradigm of Machine Translation. This can be justified by many reasons, such as accuracy, scalability, computational efficiency and fast adaptation to new languages and domains. Seeking better translation quality, SMT has evolved from the IBM word-based models (Brown et al. 1990) to phrase-based models (PBSMT) (Koehn et al. 2003). However, Phrase-based SMT lacks the capability of producing more grammatical translations and handling long-range reordering while maintaining the grammatical structure of the translation output. A more challenging aspect of Statistical Machine Translation from Arabic to English lies in bringing the Arabic source morpho-syntax to bear on the lexical as well as word-order choices of the English target string.

The main objective of this chapter is introducing our work for extending Phrase-based SMT systems with syntactic structures to provide more grammatical translations and better reordering without compromising the advantages of such systems. Recently, SMT researchers started to focus on extending Phrase-based

SMT systems with syntactic knowledge; however, the previous techniques have limited capabilities due to introducing redundantly ambiguous syntactic structures and using decoders with limited language models, and with a high computational cost.

In this chapter, we present two main contributions: first, a novel model of Phrase-based SMT which integrates linguistic lexical descriptions supertags into the target language model and the target side of the translation model. Second, a novel Incremental Dependency-based Syntactic Language Model (IDLM) based on wide-coverage Combinatory Categorial Grammar (CCG) incremental parsing which we integrate into a direct translation SMT system. Our proposed approach is the first to integrate full dependency parsing in SMT systems with a very attractive computational cost.

This chapter is organized as follows: Section 2 introduces previous work for adding syntactic knowledge into PBSMT. Section 3 motivates the lexical syntax approach for SMT, Section 4 introduces an overview of lexical syntax and lexicalized grammars, Section 5 introduces the concept of lexical syntax for SMT and explores how we incorporate supertagged translation model and supertagged n-gram language model into Phrase-based SMT, Section 6 introduces a novel incremental dependency-based language model based on an incremental version of CCG, Section 7 introduces our novel Dependency-based Direct Translation Model(DDTM), and finally Section 8 concludes and discusses future research direction.

2. Related work

Recently, researchers started to investigate how to incorporate syntactic knowledge into PBSMT system to improve the translation quality. (Chiang 2005) introduced an approach for incorporating syntax into Phrase-based SMT, targeting mainly phrase reordering. This was the first work to demonstrate any improvement when adding hierarchical structure to Phrase-based SMT. In this approach, hierarchical phrase transduction probabilities are used to handle a range of reordering phenomena in the correct fashion.

(Marcu et al. 2006) presented two similar extensions of Phrase-based SMT systems with syntactic structure on the target language side. (Zollmann & Venugopal 2006) extended the work introduced in (Chiang 2005) by augmenting the hierarchical phrases with syntactic categories derived from parsing the target side of a parallel corpus. They associate a target parse tree for each training sentence pair with a search lattice constructed from the existing phrase translations on the corresponding source sentence. Similar to (Chiang 2005), a chart-based parser with a limited language model is used.

3. Lexical syntax for phrase based SMT

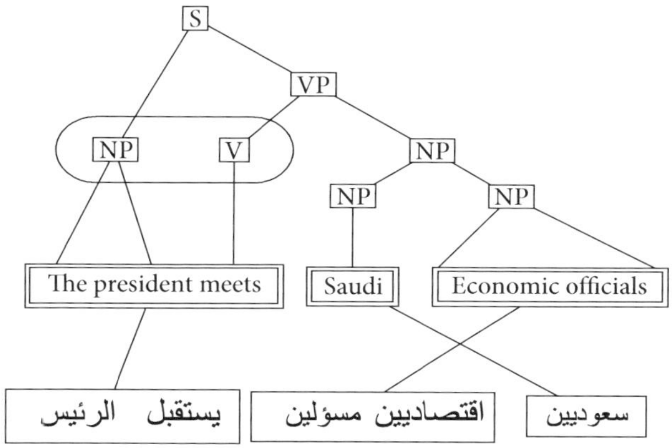

Figure 1. Inconsistent syntactic structure between Arabic and English aligned sentence pair

One major difficulty in extending PBSMT systems with linguistically motivated syntax is the mismatch between the notion of a 'phrase' in PBSMT systems (any sequence of words defined by word-alignment mapping) and the notion of a syntactic constituent in traditional linguistics. We present an example in Figure 1, which demonstrates clearly that while the first Arabic-English[1] chunk alignment contains both the English subject NP as well as the main verb *"The president meets"*, this is not conventionally accepted as a constituent in English syntax (cf. oval in the figure). In contrast, in the same example, we see that the part of the object NP *"economic officials"* – the third English chunk which maps to the second Arabic chunk – is usually interpreted as a constituent in English syntax. The problem is that the phrases in PBSMT systems are identified with regard to word alignment probabilities which need not follow any linguistic constraints.

Figure 2 exemplifies the problem of associating a tree structure with non-constituent phrases such as those commonly assumed in treebanks and existing parsers. If we tried to associate a subtree with the non-constituent phrase *"The president meets"*, the subtree must also include the three encircled nodes in the figure. These three nodes constitutes an object *NP* (marked obj) and two adjuncts (a *PP* and the other encircled *NP*). Generally speaking, any of the sentences accepted by the regular expression (`The president meets NP [PP]* [NP]*`) that occur in the training data will imply a new subtree for the phrase in question. The resulting subtrees differ only with respect to the number of adjuncts included

1. Arabic written from left to right for convenience.

under the *VP.* We refer to this as redundant syntactic ambiguity, because these subtrees unnecessarily partition the contexts and statistics of this phrase. Such redundancy represents an obstacle for any generalization to new instances and complicates the model both statistically and computationally.

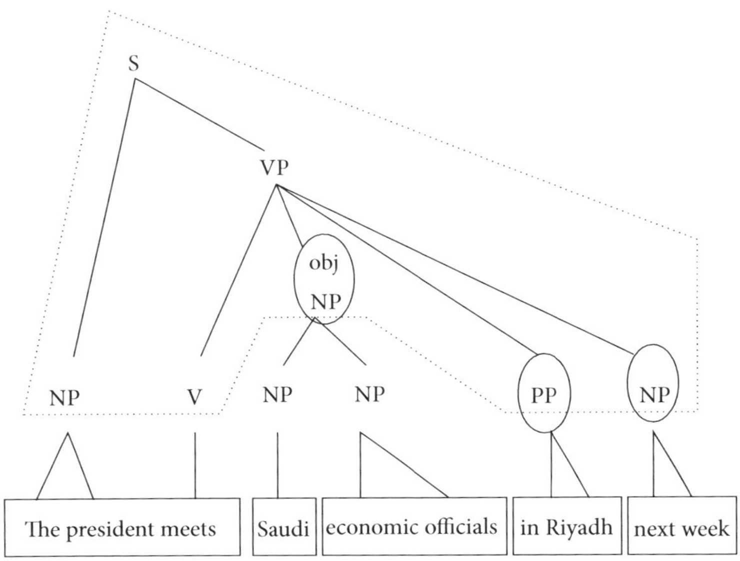

Figure 2. Mismatch between PBSMT phrases and tree structures

Due to such mismatches, it is not directly clear how the SMT notion of a phrase may be extended with a *tree* structure without introducing redundant ambiguity. For a non-constituent phrase, a tree structure representation directly introduces redundant ambiguity; multiple, alternative subtrees will be associated with the same phrase, whereas they are merely minor variants of each other, differing only in subgraphs that denote very specific contexts of the phrase.

The alternative, therefore, is to look for syntactic descriptions that do not produce redundant ambiguity in the phrase translation pairs. These syntactic descriptions must ensure an adequate and efficient representation of syntactic constraints on the word/lexeme level; moreover, these syntactic descriptions should be able to localize the global dependencies on the local, word/lexeme level. Accordingly, we explore a syntactic localization of PBSMT systems based on lexicon-driven approaches to linguistic syntax, i.e. Lexicalized Tree-Adjoining Grammar (Bangalore & Joshi 1999) and Combinatory Categorial Grammar (Steedman 2000). In these linguistic approaches, it is assumed that the grammar consists of a very rich lexicon and a small set of combinatory operators that assemble lexical entries together into parse-trees. These operators neither carry nor presuppose further linguistic knowledge beyond what the lexicon contains. The lexical entries consist of syntactic constructs (supertags) that describe such lexical information as the POS tag of the word, its sub-categorization information and the hierarchy of phrase categories that the word projects upwards in the parse-tree.

In the next section, we briefly overview the Lexical Syntax paradigm.[2]

4. Lexical syntax overview

Modern linguistic theory proposes Lexicalized Grammar in which a syntactic parser has access to an extensive lexicon of word – structure pairs and a small set of operations to manipulate and combine the lexical entries into parses. Examples of formal instantiations of this idea include Lexicalized Tree Adjoining Grammar (LTAG) (Bangalore & Joshi 1999) and Combinatory Categorial Grammar (Steedman 2000). The lexical entries are syntactic constructs that specify information such as POS tag, sub-categorization/dependency information and other syntactic constraints at the level of agreement features. Lexicalized grammar encodes the dependency, syntactic and semantic information on the lexical level; such that the grammar localizes long distance dependencies. These characteristics turned out to be pivotal for integrating syntax into SMT systems as we will discuss in this chapter. In this section, we review two lexicalized grammars: LTAG and CCG. Both have been used in the work described in this chapter.

4.1 Lexicalized Tree Adjoining Grammar

In Lexicalized Tree Adjoining Grammar (LTAG) (Bangalore & Joshi 1999) a lexical description is an elementary tree structure. Each elementary tree represents a possible tree structure for the word. There are two kinds of elementary trees, initial trees and auxiliary trees. The elementary tree represents a complex syntax description that localizes the syntactic and semantics constrains using sub-categorization (predicate/argument) information. Elementary trees can be combined using two operations, substitution and adjunction. Substitution is used to attach an initial tree while adjunction is used to attach an auxiliary one.

2. The reader is referred to (Hassan 2009) for a thorough account of Lexical Syntax.

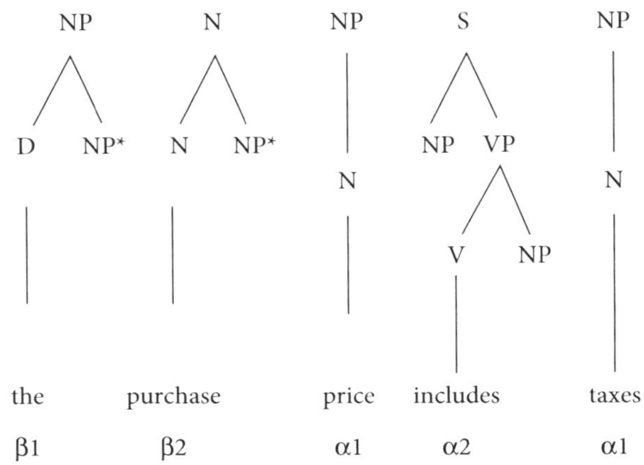

Figure 3. An LTAG supertag sequence for the sentence

As shown in the example in Figure 3, LTAG supertag is an elementary tree structure, the LTAG sub-categorization information is most clearly available in the verb *includes* which takes a subject NP to its left and an object NP to its right.

4.2 LTAG supertagging

The term "supertagging" (Bangalore & Joshi 1999) refers to tagging each of the words of a sentence with a supertag which represent the elementary tree associated with the lexical item. When well-formed, an ordered sequence of supertags can be viewed as a compact representation of a small set of constituents/parses that can be obtained by assembling the supertags together using the appropriate combinatory operators (such as substitution and adjunction in LTAG). Similar to POS tagging, the process of *supertagging* an input utterance proceeds with statistics that are based on the probability of a word-supertag pair given their Markovian or local context. This is the main difference with full parsing: supertagging the input utterance need not result in a fully connected graph; hence "almost" parsing.

4.3 Combinatory Categorial Grammar

Combinatory Categorial Grammar (CCG) (Steedman 2000) is a lexicalized grammatical theory based on Categorial Grammar. The CCG lexical entries define syntactic categories which encode syntactic valency and directionality; these categories can be augmented by a semantic representation to provide compositional semantics with a completely transparent interface between surface syntax and logical semantics. Although in this chapter we focus on syntactic structures, CCG provides the possibility of expanding the work presented in this chapter to semantic representation as well.

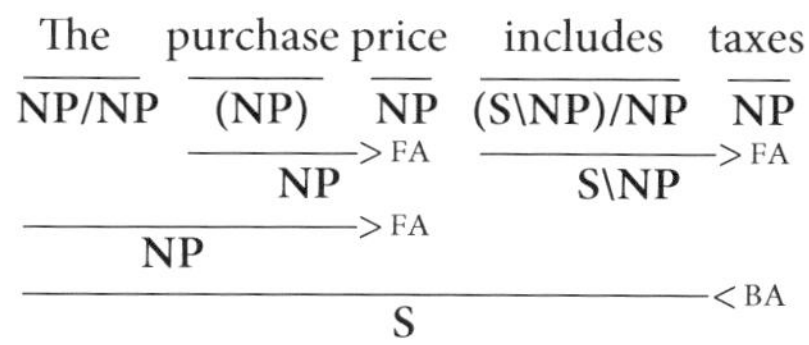

Figure 4. CCG supertags and the derivation combining the supertags into a parse-tree

Each word is associated with syntactic categories which define its syntactic behavior in different contexts. There are two kinds of syntactic categories: atomic categories and complex categories. Atomic categories are simple categories like S, NP, PP and N. Complex categories are functors; for example a complex category like X/Y will take argument Y to result in category X.

The example in Figure 4 shows a sentence with CCG supertags that combine into parse derivations using combinator operators. For example the verb "includes" has a category of a transitive verb that requires an NP to the left as its subject and an NP to the right as its object.

(Clark & Curran 2007) introduced a CCG supertagger based on log-linear probabilities that condition a supertag on a vector of features representing its context. This supertagger is trained under the Maximum-Entropy framework.

4.4 Comparison between LTAG and CCG

The CCG Combinatory Operators assemble lexical entries together into derivation-trees; each partial or complete syntactic derivation corresponds directly to a structure. For example, strings such as "*John likes*" have a natural interpretation as constituents. Therefore, the flexibility of CCG derivations allows the handling of non-constituent constructions that LTAG cannot handle, which is due to the fact that LTAG trees represent rigid structures while CCG categories allow more flexibility in the derivation process. Unlike many other linguistic theories, this flexibility gives CCG an advantage over other grammatical formalisms in handling non-constituent constructions.

5. Supertagged PBSMT

Lexical syntax deploys rich syntax descriptions, supertags, that match individual words, and a limited set of Combinatory Operators which are used to combine supertags into a set of constituents/derivations. The supertagging language model replaces the set of Combinatory Operators with the more robust and efficient, statistical *n*-gram language model over the sequence of supertags (thus *'almost parsing')*. Supertagging language model can be implemented using finite-state technology, e.g. Markov Models (Bangalore & Joshi 1999). In such finite-state representation, the syntactic structure probability is approximated as a sequence of probabilities based on the local context of the supertags.

Supertagging has two very interesting properties which make it especially suitable for extending PBSMT with syntax. Firstly, a supertag sequence can be constructed for any phrase found in a text, whether the phrase corresponds to a syntactic constituent or not. This implies that the target side of the phrase pairs can be augmented by supertags in a straightforward manner by annotating the parallel corpus with supertag sequences. Secondly, a supertag provides an extended *lexical* description of the neighborhood and dependents of a word. Therefore, co-occurrence statistics over supertags may provide a good approximation of the syntactic validity of a concatenation of two phrases, leading to more fluent output.

This work is described in detail in our previous work in (Hassan et al. 2007) where we added work on CCG, used larger data sets, used a different decoder, showed greater improvements, as well as providing details on possible upper bounds with the method, and discussions on how the two supertaggers might be combined into one model; and finally, our work in (Hassan et al. 2008a) provided detailed experiments and a more thorough analysis of the system.

We extend the baseline model (Hoang & Koehn 2008) with lexical syntactic representations (*supertags*) both in the language model as well as in the phrase translation model. A supertag represents a complex, linguistic word category that encodes a syntactic structure expressing a specific local behavior of a word, in terms of the arguments it takes (e.g. subject, object) and the syntactic environment in which it appears.

Three aspects make supertags attractive in the context of SMT. Firstly, supertags are rich syntactic constructs that exist for individual words and so it is straightforward to integrate them into SMT models that deploy phrases with arbitrary boundaries (constituents or non-constituents). Secondly, supertags are defined on a word level, which fits well with sequential (finite state) statistical models. Finally, because supertags are rich lexical descriptions that localize global syntactic constraints, it is possible to gain some of the benefits of the syntactic constraints without the huge cost of full parsing.

5.1 A supertag-based SMT model

Our extension of the baseline includes supertags both in the phrase translation table and in the language model. As for the translation table, we employ the aforementioned supertaggers to enrich the English side of the parallel training corpus with the 1-best supertag sequence per sentence. Then we extract phrase pairs together with the co-occurring English supertag sequence from this corpus using the same phrase extraction method used in the baseline model. For each extracted lexical phrase pair, we extract the corresponding supertagged phrase pairs from the supertagged target sequence in the training corpus. For each lexical phrase pair, there is at least one corresponding supertagged phrase pair, i.e. a phrase pair in which the target phrase is supertagged.

As for the supertagged language model, we employ the two aforementioned supertaggers to provide supertags sequences for a very large monolingual English corpus, from which we acquire an HMM supertagger based on a 5-gram language model over supertags. This provides us with two HMM supertagging systems (CCG and LTAG) which are trained on large monolingual target language data. This reduces the problems of sparseness in the lexical model, and provides useful language model probabilities for integration within our supertagged PBSMT model, described in the next section. The mathematical formulation of the model is discussed in detail in (Hassan et al. 2008a; Hassan 2009).

5.2 Decoder

The decoder used in this work is Moses (Hoang & Koehn 2008), a log-linear decoder which we modified to accommodate supertag phrase probabilities and supertag language models. It is worth noting that while Moses implements factored translation models, in this work we do not utilize the factored translation functionality.

5.3 Experiments

In this section we evaluate the effect of supertagged models on the translation quality. A number of experiments were carried out on the NIST open domain news translation task from Arabic to English, with the aim of examining the effect of incorporating both supertagging approaches (CCG or LTAG) in our models with varying data sizes.

5.3.1 *Data and settings*

The systems were trained on the LDC Arabic-English parallel corpus; we used the news part (130K sentences, about 5 million words)[3] to train systems with what we call the *small* data set, and the news together with a large part of the UN

3. LDC2004T17 and LDC2004T18.

data[4] (2 million sentences, about 50 million words) for experiments with *large* data sets.

The *n*-gram target LM and the supertag LM were built using 250M words from the English GigaWord Corpus using the SRILM toolkit[5] For the LTAG supertags experiments, we used the LTAG English supertagger (Bangalore & Joshi 1999) to tag the English part of the parallel data and the monolingual LM data. For the CCG supertag experiments, we used the CCG supertagger in the 'C&C' tools[6] to tag the English part of the parallel corpus as well as the CCG supertag LM data.

5.3.2 *Baseline vs. Supertags on small data sets*

The baseline system is a state-of-the-art PBSMT system as described in (Koehn et al. 2003). We built two baseline systems with two different-sized training sets: 'Base-SMALL' (5 million words) and 'Base-LARGE' (50 million words) as described in the previous section. Both systems use a 5-gram language model with Kneser-Ney discounting built using 250 million words from the English GigaWord Corpus.

We compared the translation quality of the baseline systems with the LTAG and CCG supertags systems (LTAG-SMALL and CCG-SMALL). The results are given in Table 1. All systems were trained on the same parallel data. The LTAG supertag-based system outperforms the baseline by 2.44 BLEU points absolute (or 6.1% relative), while the CCG supertag-based system scores 1.66 BLEU points over the baseline (4.1% relative). These statistically significant improvements indicate that the rich information in supertags helps select better translation candidates.

Table 1. LTAG and CCG systems on small data

System	BLEU score
Base-SMALL	40.08
LTAG-SMALL	42.52
CCG-SMALL	41.74

5.3.3 *Scalability: Larger training corpora*

Outperforming a PBSMT system on small amounts of training data is less impressive than doing so on really large data sets. The issues here concern scalability as

4. LDC2004E13.

5. http://www. speech, sri.com/projects/srilm/

6. http://svn.ask.it.usyd.edu.au/trac/candc

well as the question as to whether the PBSMT system is able to bridge the performance gap with the supertagged system when reasonably large sizes of training data are used. To this end, we trained the systems on 2 million sentences of parallel data, deploying LTAG supertags and CCG supertags. Table 2 presents the comparison between these systems and the baseline trained on the same data. The LTAG system improves by 1.82 BLEU points (4.1% relative), but the CCG system gives an even larger increase: 1.91 BLEU points (4.3% relative). While the relative improvement score for CCG is a little higher than with the smaller data set, for LTAG it is slightly lower (6.1% on the smaller data set). Nonetheless, the fact that sustained increases are to be found at all is probably due to observing more data with different supertag contexts, which enables the models to select better target language phrases.

Table 2. Performance on large training data

System	BLEU score
Base-LARGE	44.18
LTAG-LARGE	46.00
CCG-LARGE	**46.09**

5.3.4 *Systems output analysis*

In order to acquire a deeper insight into the effect of the supertag components on system output, as well as where they might not help, we conducted a manual analysis of a subset of the system's output against the baseline and reference translations. We picked a number of sentences where the translations of the baseline system and the supertagged systems are significantly different. We performed human analysis for the translation to understand the supertags effect.

Table 3. How CCG improves over baseline

N = 50 test sentences		
Reason	**#**	**%**
Inserting verb omitted by baseline	11	22%
Better reordering	11	22%
Better word/phrase selection	5	10%
Other reasons	23	46%

Table 3 exhibits the reasons for improved output for the CCG-based system over the baseline system. Only 22% of the cases are due to improved reordering, mainly verb/subject and noun/adjective, as illustrated in Figure 5. The CCG system correctly includes a verb which was omitted by the baseline system in 22% of cases; this concerns verbs such as *said, concluded, is, signed*, etc., as shown in Figure 6.

Source: من جانبه ، قال ايفانوف ان العلاقات الروسية ـ الصينية شهدت تقدمًا ملحوظًا خلال الاعوَام الماضية

Reference: *For his part, Ivanov said that Sino-Russian relations have undergone marked progress in recent years.*

Baseline: *For his part, said Ivanov that russian-chinese relations witnessed a remarkable progress during the past years.*

CCG: *For his part, Ivanov said that russian-chinese relations witnessed a remarkable progress during the past years.*

Figure 5. Improved reordering in the CCG system

Omitting verbs turns out to be a problem for the baseline system; however, both supertagged systems have a more grammatically strict language model than a standard word-level Markov model, and so exhibit a preference (in the CCG system especially) for the insertion of a verb with a similar meaning to that contained in the reference sentence.

Source: واجرَى عنان تحقيقًا داخليًا في فبراير لكنه الغاه في مارس تمهيدًا لتحقيق اوسع ومستقل

Reference: *Annan opened an internal investigation in February but cancelled it in March in preparation for a broader, independent investigation.*

Baseline: *Annan was to internally in February but abolished in March as a prelude to broader and independent.*

CCG: *Annan conducted an internal inquiry in February but abolished in March in preparation for broader and independent.*

Figure 6. Overcoming missing verbs in the CCG system

Apart from improvements with these verbs, the CCG system achieves better output due to improved word/phrase selection in about 10% of the cases. In a large number (48%) of cases, the CCG system improvement is accounted for by a number of reasons, e.g. selecting the correct form of verb, restoring negation, improved grammaticality, and a variety of other reasons.

In general we observed that supertagging seems to help most when the baseline system already has reasonable alternative translations; where supertagging improves the selection of a better translation.

While on average our system selects more grammatical output than the baseline, it is still limited to the same set of hypothesis translations that can be built by the standard reordering mechanism used in the baseline system. There are reasons to believe that the set of hypotheses can be improved upon by more advanced, syntax-driven reordering techniques. Nonetheless, our supertags-based Arabic-English system described in (Hassan et al. 2007b) was ranked first by some margin in the human evaluation, despite this clear advantage of more readable output not carrying over to the automatic evaluation scores.

Having addressed the question as to whether lexical syntax can be of use in PBSMT, we now move our attention to the related questions of whether lexical syntax can provide PBSMT with full parsing capability and whether this is needed by PBSMT systems. We will try to answer these questions in the next sections.

6. Dynamic Syntactic Language Model

In the previous section, we showed our supertagged PBSMT model which integrated supertags into translation model and an *n*-gram supertags language model into a baseline PBSMT system; this integration significantly improved the translation accuracy. However, there is no guarantee that the sequence of proposed supertagged phrases constructs a valid syntactic constituent. Another more serious, though expected, drawback is that supertags language models cannot handle long-range dependencies. In this section, we introduce a solution for those problems: a syntactic language model that enables the integration of incremental parsing seamlessly into PBSMT systems. In the next section, we will show how our proposed DSLM is integrated into the PBSMT system.

6.1 From supertagging to syntax-based language model

In the previous section, we deployed the supertagging language model to PBSMT. Originally, *'almost parsing'* had been proposed for handling monolingual strings, where the given sequence of words already constructs a presumed syntactic structure (Bangalore & Joshi 1999). In the bilingual (machine translation) case, the sequence of candidate target words might not construct a valid syntactic structure nor a compelling sequence of associated supertags; therefore, achieving *'almost parsing'* by deploying a supertags *n*-gram language model on the huge space of hypotheses, representing the candidate translations, is more challenging in the machine translation case than in the monolingual parsing case.

We argue that the MT case needs a more sophisticated mechanism that can satisfy three important aspects. First, it needs to efficiently support long-range dependencies and construct full parse structures such that it would enable the MT system to distinguish between different candidate phrases based on their role in constructing the parse structure and satisfying the syntactic dependencies. Second, as is widely known, PBSMT systems produce the translation candidates incrementally by processing source words from left-to-right in a Markov fashion; therefore, the mechanism should comply with this incremental method. Third, the mechanism should be computationally efficient such that it can be integrated into large-scale PBSMT systems.

In this section, we introduce a syntax-based language model which deploys a CCG incremental parsing mechanism to construct the parsing structure step-by-step, where each step represents the accumulation of parsing decisions as the parser *dynamically* consumes the input word-by-word from left-to-right. The proposed syntax-based language model complies with the Markovian nature of PBSMT decoders; therefore, it has the potential to be integrated seamlessly with such systems. Furthermore, it is based on a deterministic parsing approach, i.e. it maintains a limited number of parse decisions at each parsing step which makes it very computationally efficient. In the next section we will briefly introduce our proposed Dynamic Syntactic Language Model (DSLM).

6.2 DSLM Overview

We propose a dynamic model of syntax in which the syntactic process is represented by a sequence of transitions between adjacent syntactic/semantic states. The syntactic representation is built step-by-step from left-to-right while traversing the input string as shown in (1).

$$S_0 \xrightarrow{w_1} S_1 \xrightarrow{w_2} S_2 \cdots\cdots\cdots\cdots S_{n-1} \xrightarrow{w_n} S_n \tag{1}$$

Our DSLM is an embodiment of the theoretical representation outlined above, where we use an incremental parser based on CCG as the grammatical representation of the syntactic/semantic states and the transition actions that lead from a state to another. As shown in (2), each word w_i is associated with a lexical syntactic/semantic descriptor st_i. At each transition, a parsing action o_i is associated with that transition, which transforms the current parsing state S_i to the next state S_{i+1} which, in turn, represents a new partial syntactic derivation. When the last word is encountered, a final state S_n represents the final syntactic structure for the given sequence of words. Such a sequence of parsing actions constructs the parsing derivation step-by-step.

$$S_0 \xrightarrow[w_1,\, st_1]{o_1} S_1 \xrightarrow[w_2,\, st_2]{o_2} S_2 \cdots\cdots\cdots\cdots S_i \xrightarrow[w_i,\, st_i]{o_i} S_{i+1} \cdots\cdots\cdots\cdots S_n \tag{2}$$

We use incremental CCG as our grammatical representation such that the lexical descriptor st_i is represented by a CCG supertag, the parsing action o_i is represented by a CCG Combinatory Operator with the state S_i being a composite CCG category.

In the remainder of this section, we will describe the mechanics of this incremental parser, while the deployment of DSLM in machine translation systems will be introduced in Section 7.

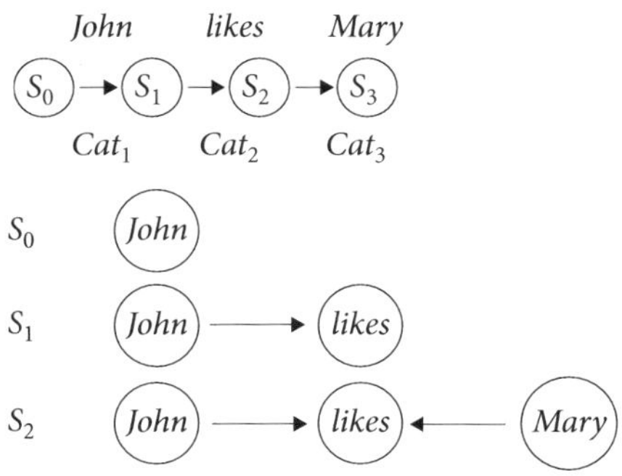

Figure 7. Illustration of the incremental parser representation and the associated intermediate dependency graphs at each state

6.3 Incremental parsing for CCG

The incremental parsing process consists of the construction of such dependency graphs in a step-by-step manner. An incremnetal parser usuauly faces the problem of keeping the incremntality as well as being determinstic (Nivre 2004).

Figure 7 illustrates the incremental parsing representation. The proposed approach deploys three modules in a cascade: (1) a statistical *Supertagger,* (2) a statistical *Operator tagger,* and (3) a deterministic *Parsing State Realizer.*

Figure 8 is an example of the workings of this parser. Practically speaking, after POS tagging the input sentence, the parser employs two components: (i) a Supertag-Operator Tagger which proposes a supertag-operator pair for the current word, and (ii) a deterministic State-Realizer, which realizes the current state by applying the current operator to the previous state and the current supertag.

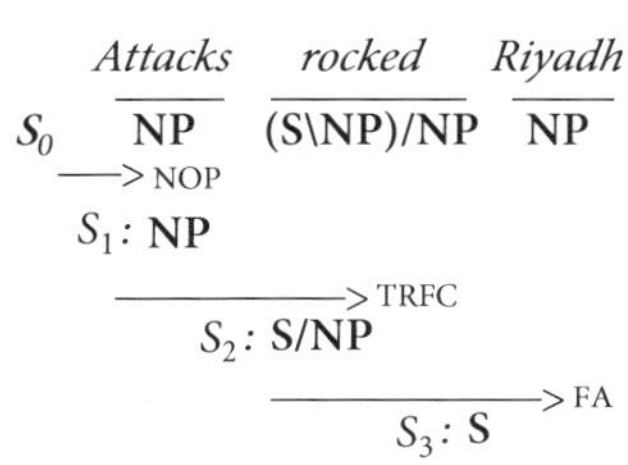

Figure 8. Supertag-, operator- and state-sequences. NOP: No Operation; TRFC: Type Raise-Forward Composition; FA: Forward Application. The CCG operators show that `Attacks` and `Riyadh` are both dependents of `rocked`.

6.3.1 *Supertag-Operator Tagger*

The Supertag-Operator Tagger implements the probability $P(W, S)$ of a word sequence $W = w_1^n$ and a parse-state sequence $S = s_1^n$, with the associated supertag sequence $ST = st_1^n$ and operator sequence $O = o_1^n$, which represents a possible derivation. Given a supertag st_i and an operator o_i, the state S_i is calculated deterministically by the State-Realizer. This model is described in (3):

$$P(W,S) = \prod_{i=1}^{n} \overbrace{P(w_i \mid W_{i-1} S_{i-1})}^{\text{Word Predictor}} \times \overbrace{P(st_i \mid W_i)}^{\text{Supertagger}} \times \overbrace{P(o_i \mid W_i, S_{i-1}, ST_i)}^{\text{Operator Tagger}} \quad (3)$$

In (3):

- $P(w_i \mid W_{i-1} S_{i-1})$ is the probability of w_i given the previous sequence of words W_{i-1} and the previous sequence of states S_{i-1}.
- $P(st_i \mid W_i)$: is the probability of the supertag st_i given the word sequence W_i up to the current position. Basically, this represents a sequence tagger (a 'supertagger').
- $P(o_i \mid W_i, S_{i-1}, ST_i)$ represents the probability of the operator o_i given the previous words, state sequences and supertags up to the current position. This represents a CCG operator tagger.

It is worth noting that the proposed language model parser is deterministic, in the sense that it maintains a limited number of parsing states, only one here, that represent possible parsing decisions at each word position. This characteristic is very important for incorporating DSLM into large-scale MT systems due to the computational efficiency.

The supertagger and the operator tagger have to be trained on left-to-right incremental CCG derivations. In order to obtain such data, we transformed the CCGbank (Hockenmaier 2003) from normal form derivations to strictly left-to-right derivations that can satisfy the dependencies in the CCGbank. Our original approach for inducing incremental derivations from the normal form derivations in CCGBank is described in detail in (Hassan et al. 2009; Hassan 2009). A more formalized approach for inducing incremental derivations from CCGBank has been introduced in (Hefny et al. 2011).

7. Dependency-based Direct Translation Model (DDTM)

In this section we introduce a novel Dependency Direct Translation Model (DDTM) with target-language syntax while maintaining linear-time decoding.

This model presents a framework for SMT that works with a rich discriminative model and incremental dependency parsing, without necessarily resorting to synchronous grammars between languages of different syntactic structures, as is the case of Arabic and English. In our model, the synchronized productions are encoded implicitly in the conditional translation probabilities that involve an extended source Arabic morpho-syntactic feature set and the partial target syntactic structure built so far.

The Direct Translation Model (DTM) (Papineni et al. 1997) employs the *a posteriori* conditional distribution $P(T|S)$ of a target sentence T given a source sentence S. As opposed to the common inversion into $P(S|T)$ based on the noisy-channel approach (Brown et al. 1990), DTM2 (Ittycheriah & Roukos 2007) expresses the phrase-based translation task in a unified probabilistic, log-linear framework consisting of three components:

- A prior conditional distribution $P_0(.|S)$,
- A number of feature functions $\phi_i()$ that capture the translation and language model effects, and
- The weights of the features λ_i, estimated under Maximum Entropy framework

The log-linear formulation of DTM2 is shown in Equation (4)

$$P(T,J|S)=\frac{P_0(T,J|S)}{Z}\exp\sum_i \lambda_i\,\phi_i(T,J,S) \qquad (4)$$

Here Z is the per source sentence normalization term. J is the sequence of skip reordering factors for the phrase pairs captured by $\phi_i()$, which represents the sequence of jumps from one source word position to the next (for details see (Ittycheriah & Roukos 2007). The prior probability P_0 is the prior distribution for the phrase probability which is estimated using the phrase normalized counts commonly used in conventional PBSMT systems (e.g. (Koehn et al. 2003)).

DTM2 differs from other PBSMT models in that it extracts from a word-aligned parallel corpus only a *non-redundant* set of *minimal phrases* in the sense that no two phrases overlap with each other.

Baseline DTM2 Features: The baseline employs a language model, and the following four types of features:

- *Lexical Micro Features* examining source and target words in the phrases (i.e. possible tarnslations for the current source word),
- *Lexical Context Features* encoding the source and target phrase contexth (i.e. previous and next source words, and previous target words within a defined window),

- *Source Morphological Features* encoding morphological and segmentation characteristics of source words. This feature can model the morphological variations of Arabic source words.
- *Part-of-Speech Features* encoding source and target POS tags as well as the POS tags of the surrounding contexts of phrases,

The DTM2 approach based on MaxEnt provides a flexible framework for incorporating other available feature types as we demonstrate below.

DTM2 Decoder: The decoder for the baseline is a beam search decoder similar to decoders used in standard log-linear PBSMT systems such as (Koehn et al. 2003). The main difference between the DTM2 decoder and the standard PBSMT decoders is that DTM2 deploys Maximum Entropy probabilistic models to obtain the translation costs and various feature costs by deploying the features described above in a discriminative MaxEnt fashion.

7.1 Model overview

In this section we extend the DTM2 model with incremental target dependency-based syntax. We call the resulting model the Dependency-based Direct Translation Model (DDTM). This extension takes place by (i) extracting syntactically enriched minimal phrase pairs, (ii) including a new set of syntactic feature functions among the exponential model features, and (iii) adapting the decoder for dealing with syntax, including various pruning strategies and enhancements. Next we describe each extension in turn.

7.2 Phrase table: Incremental syntax

The target-side sentences in the word-aligned parallel corpus used for training are parsed using the incremental dependency parser described in (Hassan et al. 2009). This results in a word-aligned parallel corpus where the words of the target sentences are tagged with supertags and operators. From this corpus we extract the set of minimal phrase pairs using the method described in (Ittycheriah & Roukos 2007), extracting along with every target phrase the associated sequences of supertags and operators. As shown in (5), a source phrase $s_1, \ldots, s_n$ translates into a target phrase $w_1, \ldots, w_m$ where every word w_i is labeled with a supertag st_i, and a possible accompanying parsing operator o_i in the parsed parallel corpus:

$$s_1, \ldots, s_n \longrightarrow [w_1, st_1, o_1], \ldots, [w_m, st_m, o_m] \quad (5)$$

Accordingly, our phrase table associates with every target phrase an *incremental parsing – possibly not fully connected – subgraph*. These subgraphs along with their probabilities represent our phrase table augmented with incremental dependency parsing structure.

This representation turns the complicated problem of MT with parsing into a sequential classification problem in which the classifier deploys various features from the source sentence and the candidate target translations to specify a sequence of decisions that finally results in an output target string along with its associated dependency graph. The classification decisions are performed in sequence step-by-step while traversing the input string to provide decisions on possible words, supertags, operators and states. A beam search decoder simultaneously decides which sequence is the most probable.

7.3 DDTM features

The exponential model and the MaxEnt framework used in DTM2 and DDTM enabled us to explore the utility of incremental syntactic parsing within a rich feature space. In our DDTM system, we implemented a set of features alongside the baseline DTM2 features that were discussed in (Ittycheriah & Roukos 2007). The features described here encode all the probabilistic components in (3) within a log-linear interpretation along with some more empirically intuitive features.

- Supertag-Word features: these features examine the target phrase words with their associated supertags, and are related to the Supertagger component in (3).
- Supertag sequence features: these features encode *n*-gram supertags (equivalent to the *n*-gram supertags Language Model). This feature is also related to the Supertagger component.
- Supertag-Operator features: these features encode supertags and associated operators, which are related to the Operator Tagger component in (3).
- Supertag-State features: these features register state and supertag co-occurrences.
- State sequence features: these features encode *n*-gram state features and are equivalent to an *n*-gram Language Model over parse state sequences, which is related to the multiplication in (3).
- Word-State sequence features: these features encode word and state co-occurrences, which are related to the Word Predictor component in (3).

The exponential model and the MaxEnt framework used in DTM2 and DDTM enable us to explore the utility of incremental syntactic parsing with the use of minimal phrases within a rich feature space.

7.4 DDTM decoder

In order to support incremental dependency parsing, we extend the DTM2 decoder in three ways: firstly, by constructing the syntactic states during decoding; secondly, by extending the hypothesis structures to incorporate the syntactic states and the partial dependency derivations; and thirdly, by modifying the pruning strategy to handle the large search space. At decoding time, each hypothesis state is associated with a parse-state which is constructed while decoding using the incremental parsing approach introduced in (Hassan et al. 2009). The previous state, the sequences of supertags and CCG incremental operators are deployed in a deterministic manner to realize the parse-states as well as the intermediate dependency graphs between words.

Figure 9 shows the DDTM decoder while decoding a sentence with the English translation "Attacks rocked Riyadh". Each hypothesis is associated with a parse-state S_i and a partial dependency graph (shown for some states only, for reasons of space). Moreover, each transition is associated with an operator *o* that combines the previous state and the current supertag *st* to construct the next state S_i. The decoder starts from a null state S_1 and then proceeds with a possible expansion with the word "attacks", supertag *NP* and operator *NOP* to produce the next hypothesis with state S_2 and category *NP*. Further expansion for that path with

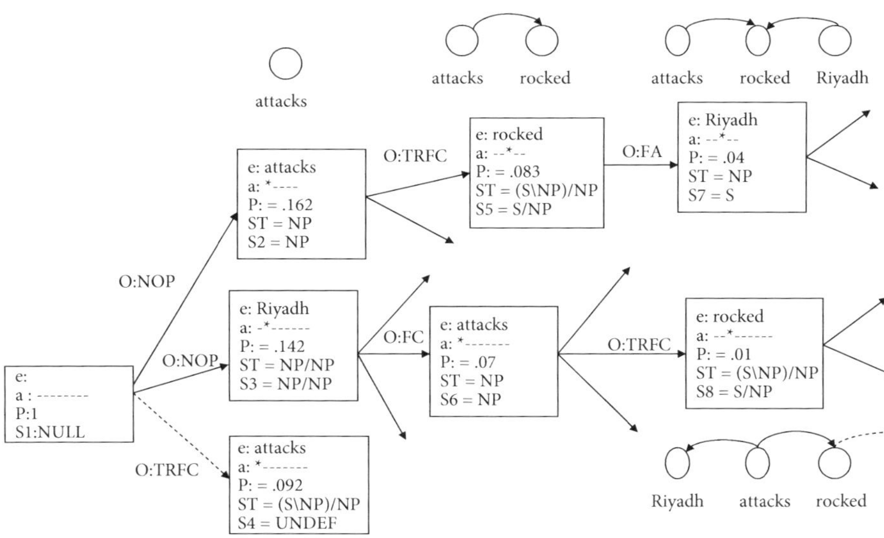

Figure 9. DDTM decoder operation for the sentence "Attacks rocked Riyadh". Each hypothesis has a parse state and a partial dependency structure

the verb "rocked", supertag *(S\NP)/NP* and operator *TRFC* will produce the state S_5 with category *S/NP*. The partial dependency graph for state S_5 is shown above the state where a dependency relation between the two words is established. Furthermore, another expansion with the word "Riyadh", supertag *NP* and operator *FA* produces state S_7 with category *S* and a complete dependency graph as shown above the state. Another path which spans the states S_1, S_3, S_6 and S_8 ends with a state category *S/NP* and a partial dependency graph as shown under state S_8 where the dependency graph is still missing its object (e.g. "Riyadh attacks rocked the Saudi Govt.").

7.4.1 *Growing search space*

The addition of parse-states may result in a very large search space due to the fact that the same phrase/word may have many possible supertags and many possible operators. Moreover, the same word sequences may have many parse-state sequences and, therefore, many hypotheses that represent the same word sequence. The search space is definitely larger than the baseline search space by a factor of at least 60% compared to the baseline search space. Accordingly, we adopt some pruning heuristics to limit the search space.

Any hypothesis which does not constitute a valid parse-state is discarded, i.e. if the previous parse-state and the current supertag sequence cannot construct a valid state using the associated operator sequence, then the expansion is discarded. As shown in Figure 9, the expansion from state S_1 to state S_4 (with the dotted line) is pruned and not expanded further because the proposed expansion is the verb "attacks", supertag *(S\NP)/NP* and operator *TRFC*. Since the previous state is NULL, it cannot be combined with the verb using the *TRFC* operator. This would produce an undefined state and therefore the hypothesis is discarded.

We limit the supertag and operator variants per target phrase to a predefined number of alternatives. We tuned these thresholds using a seprate developing data set (MT03 DevSet). The supertags limit was set to four alternatives while the operators limit was set to three alternatives. We tuned these thresholds for the best accuracy while maintaining a manageable search space.

As shown in Figure 9, each word can have many alternatives with different supertags. In this example the word "attacks" has two forms, namely a noun and a verb.

Standard PBSMT decoders merge translation hypotheses if they cover the same source words and share the same *n*-gram language model history. Similarly, the DDTM decoder merges translation hypotheses if they cover the same source words, share the same *n*-gram language model history and share the same parse-state history.

7.5 Experiments

We conducted experiments on an Arabic-to-English translation task using LDC and GALE data,[7] totaling 7.8 M parallel sentences. The 5-gram language model was trained on the English Gigaword Corpus and the English part of the parallel corpus. Our baseline system is similar to the system described in (Ittycheriah & Roukos 2007). We report results on NIST MT05 and NIST MT06 evaluations test sets using BLEU and TER as automatic evaluation metrics.

To train the DDTM model, we use the incremental parser introduced in (Hassan et al. 2009) to parse the target side of the parallel training data. Each sentence is associated with supertag, operator and parse-state sequences. We then train models with different feature sets.

7.5.1 *Results*

We compared the baseline DTM2 system (Ittycheriah & Roukos 2007) with our DDTM system with the features listed in Section 7.5. We examined the effect of all features on system performance. In this set of experiments we used the 3.7 M-sentence LDC parallel data only, and the results are reported on the MT05 test set. Each of the systems examined deploy DTM2 features in addition to a number of newly added syntactic features.

Table 4. DDTM results on MT05 and MT06

System	DTM2 Baseline	DDTM
MT05 (BLEU)	55.28	55.66
MT05 (*TER*)	38.79	38.48
MT06 (BLEU)	43.56	43.91
MT06 (*TER*)	49.08	48.65

We examined a combination of the best features in our DDTM system on a larger training data comprising 7.8 M sentences from both NIST and GALE parallel corpora. Table 4 shows the results on both MT05 and MT06 test sets. As shown, DDTM outperforms the state-of-the-art baseline system, which is especially noteworthy even when very large amounts of training data are used. Despite the fact that the actual scores are not so different, we found that the baseline translation output and the DDTM translation output are significantly different. We measured this by calculating the TER between the baseline translation and the DDTM

7. LDC2006E25.

translation for the MT05 test set, and found this to be 25.9%. This large difference has not been realized by the BLEU or TER scores in comparison to the baseline. We believe that this is due to the fact that most changes that match the syntactic constraints do not bring about the best match where the automatic evaluation metrics are concerned. Accordingly, in the next section we describe the outcome of a detailed manual analysis of the output translations.

7.6 Human analysis of results

Although the BLEU score does not show a large improvement by the dependency-based system over the baseline system, human inspection of the data gives us important insights into the pros and cons of the dependency-based model. We analyzed a randomly selected set of 100 sentences from the MT05 test set. In this sample, the baseline and the DDTM system perform similarly in 64% of the sentences. It is worth noting that our DDTM system tends to produce more concise syntactic structures which may lead to a lower BLEU score due to the length penalty, despite the fact that the output may be better than the baseline.

In 28% of sentences, the DDTM system produces remarkably better translations. The examples highlighted here illustrate the behaviour of the baseline and the DDTM systems which can be observed consistently throughout the test set. Verbs are often deleted by standard PBSMT systems, but DDTM prefers to insert verbs as they have complex and more detailed syntactic structures which give better and more likely state sequences. Furthermore, the DDTM system avoids longer noun phrases and instead uses some prepositions in-between. Again, this is probably due to the fact that like verbs, prepositions have a complex syntactic description that gives rise to more likely state sequences.

On the other hand, the baseline produced better translations for 8% of the sentences in the analysis sample. The baseline does better mainly in two cases: (i) when out-of-vocabulary items or sentences which are hard to translate lead to poor syntactic structures and subsequent bad translations; and (ii) with sentences with long noun phrases, where the DDTM system prefers to introduce verbs or prepositions in the middle of such NPs – which have a relatively simple structure in CCG – with the result that the baseline produces better translations.

Figure 10 shows two examples where DDTM provides better and more concise syntactic structure. As can be seen, there is little overlap between the reference and the proposed translation. However, longer translations enhance the possibility of longer n-gram matches being selected via the BLEU score, which increases the chance of higher scores. This well-known bias does not favour the more concise output derived by our DDTM system, of course.

Source: وخضع بعد ذلك لفحوصات اجراها احد اطباء الشرطة
Reference: *He then underwent medical examinations by a police doctor.*
Baseline: *He was subjected after that tests conducted by doctors of the police.*
DDTM: *Then he underwent tests conducted by doctors of the police.*

Source: وقد هز الرياض مساء اليوم هجومان بسيارتين مفخختين
Reference: *Riyadh was rocked tonight by two car bomb attacks..*
Baseline: *Riyadh rocked today night attacks by two booby – trapped cars.*
DDTM: *Attacks rocked Riyadh today evening in two car bombs.*

Figure 10. DDTM provides better syntactic structure with more concise translations

8. Conclusion

In this chapter, we extended Phrase-based SMT with lexical syntactic description supertags that localize global syntactic information on the word level. Supertags can, therefore, be assigned to every word in a phrase without introducing syntactic redundant ambiguity. We introduced two different levels of syntactic support namely: incorporating supertagged translation model and supertagged n-gram language model into Phrase-based SMT and incorporating incremental dependency-based language model into DTM2. Both approaches proved to be useful for enhancing the translation quality and providing more grammatical translations. Future work will attempt further extensions of our DDTM system to allow for the exploitation of non-local aspects of dependency structure.

References

Bangalore, S., and A. Joshi. 1999. Supertagging: An approach to almost parsing. *Computational Linguistics* 25 (2): 237–265.

Brown, P. F., J. Cocke, S. A. Della Pietra, F. Jelinek, V. J. Della Pietra, j. D. Lafferty, R. L. Mercer, and P. S. Roossin. 1990. A statistical approach to machine translation. *Computational Linguistics* 16 (2): 79–85.

Chiang, D. 2005. A hierarchical phrase-based model for statistical machine translation. In *43rd Annual Meeting of the Association for Computational Linguistics* (ACL05), 263–270. Ann Arbor MI.

Clark, S. and J. Curran. 2007. Wide-coverage efficient statistical parsing with CCG and log-linear models. *Computational Linguistics* 33 (1): 439–552.

Hassan, H. 2009. Lexical Syntax for Statstical Machine Translation. Ph.D dissertation, Dublin City University.

Hassan, H., K. Sima'an, and A. Way. 2009. Lexicalized semi-incremental dependency parsing. In *Proceedings of RANLP 2009, the International Conference on Recent Advances in Natural Language Processing*, Borovets, Bulgaria.

Hassan, H., K. Sima'an, and A. Way. 2008a. Syntactically lexicalized phrase-based statistical translation. *IEEE Transactions on Audio, Speech and Language Processing* 6 (7): 1260–1273.

Hassan, H., K. Sima'an, and A. Way. 2007. Integrating supertags into phrase-based statistical machine translation. In Proceedings of the ACL-2007, Prague, Czech Republic, 288–295.

Hassan, H., Y. Ma, and A. Way. 2007. MATREX: The DCU machine translation system for IWSLT 2007. In *Proceedings of the 4th International Workshop on Spoken Language Translation,* 69–75. Trento, Italy.

Hoang, H., and P. Koehn. 2008. Design of the moses decoder for statistical machine translation. In *ACL Workshop on Software Engineering, Testing, and Quality Assurance for NLP 2008.*

Hefny, A., H. Hassan, and M. Bahgat. 2011. *Computational Linguistics and Intelligent Text Processing Lecture Notes in Computer Science*, Vol. 6608/2011: 96–108.

Hockenmaier, J. 2003. Data and Models for Statistical Parsing with Combinatory Categorial Grammar. Ph.D dissertation, University of Edinburgh.

Ittycheriah, A., and S. Roukos. 2007. Direct translation model 2. In *Human Language Technologies 2007: The Conference of the North American Chapter of the Association for Computational Linguistics; Proceedings of the Main Conference*, 57–64, Rochester NY.

Koehn, P., F. J. Och, and D. Marcu. 2003. Statistical phrasebased translation. In *Proceedings of the Joint Human Language Technology Conference and the Annual Meeting of the North American Chapter of the Association for Computational Linguistics* (HLT-NAACL 2003), 127–133. Edmonton AL, Canada.

Marcu, D., W. Wang, A. Echihabi, and K. Knight. 2006. SPMT: Statistical machine translation with syntactified target language phrases. In *Proceedings of the 2006 Conference on Empirical Methods in Natural Language Processing* (EMNLP 2006), 44–52, Sydney, Australia.

Nivre, J. 2004. Incrementality in deterministic dependency parsing. In *Proceedings of the ACL Workshop on Incremental Parsing: Bringing Engineering and Cognition Together*, 50–57, Barcelona, Spain.

Papineni, K., S. Roukos, and T. Ward. 1997. Feature based language understanding. In *Proceedings of 5th European Conference on Speech Communication and Technology EUROSPEECH 97*, 1435–1438, Rhodes, Greece.

Steedman, M. 2000. *The Syntactic Process*. Cambridge MA: The MIT Press.

Zollmann, A., and A. Venugopal. 2006. Syntax augmented machine translation via chart parsing. In *Proceedings of the Workshop on Statistical Machine Translation, LT/NAACL*, 138–141. New York NY.

Automatic rule induction in Arabic to English machine translation framework

Khaled Shaalan[1,2] & Ahmad Hany Hossny[3]
[1]Fellow, School of Informatics, University of Edinburgh, UK / [2]Faculty of Informatics, The British University in Dubai, UAE / [3]Centre for Intelligent Systems Research, Deakin University

This chapter addresses the exploitation of a supervised machine learning technique to automatically induce Arabic-to-English transfer rules from chunks of parallel aligned linguistic resources. The induced structural transfer rules encode the linguistic translation knowledge for converting an Arabic syntactic structure into a target English syntactic structure. These rules are going to be an integral part of an Arabic-English transfer-based machine translation. Nevertheless, a novel morphological rule induction method is employed for learning Arabic morphological rules that are applied in our Arabic morphological analyzer. To demonstrate the capability of the automated rule induction technique, we conducted rule-based translation experiments that use induced rules from a relatively small data set. The translation quality of the hybrid translation experiments achieved good results. in terms of WER.

1. Introduction

Machine translation systems incorporate two main components: the translation model and the translation engine. The translation model follows empirical (statistical or machine learning) approaches, linguistic (rule-based) approaches, or a hybrid of both. The translation engine utilizes the translation model to transform a source sentence into a target sentence. In empirical approaches, this is based on finding the most probable translation of a sentence using data gathered from an aligned bilingual corpus. Hence, some researches refer to these approaches as corpus-based. In linguistic approaches, linguistic knowledge is used in the representation of translation units. These approaches are based on linguistic analysis of the source sentence and generation of the target sentence. If the level of the analysis is not deep enough to produce a format suitable for the generation of the target language, a collection of transformations is applied to the syntactic analysis of the source language in order to construct a target-language syntactic representation. Historically, many Arabic-English machine translation systems, including commercial ones, are transfer-based. The advantages of this approach are that it can attain high performance but at the expense of the large efforts needed to build the necessary linguistic resources (Abdel Monem et al. 2008). On the other hand, corpus-based approaches require a very large parallel corpus that is neither easily available nor affordable. Nowadays, there is a growing interest in hybrid approaches. For example, a proposed approach to statistical machine translation (SMT) that combines ideas from phrase-based SMT (Koehn et al. 2003) and traditional ruled-based grammar generation (Riezler & Maxwell 2006) provides significant improvements in the grammaticality of translations over state-of-the-art phrase-based SMT on in-coverage examples, suggesting a possible hybrid framework.

In this work, we address exploiting a supervised machine learning technique to develop an example-based transfer tool that automatically induces Arabic-to-English syntactic transfer rules from chunks of parallel linguistic resources. The Arabic-English language pair is very different in morphology and syntax. The richness of Arabic morphology has led us to develop a novel morphological rule induction method for learning Arabic morphological rules that are applied in our Arabic morphological analyzer. To demonstrate the capability of these automated techniques we conducted rule-based translation experiments that use induced rules from a relatively small data set. The induced syntactic transfer rules are learned from a set of Arabic-English example pairs, each of which includes the feature structure representing the linguistic knowledge of each word. The obtained results from the evaluated hybrid system, i.e. rule-based translation system whose transfer rules have been generated using inductive techniques, were promising and assure that using the proposed machine learning technique would improve the performance of the Arabic-to-English rule-based sentence translation.

The rest of the chapter is organized as follows. Section 2 gives a brief background on inductive logic programming with regard to natural language processing tasks. Section 3 discusses some hybrid machine translation systems. Section 4 describes the related research on automatic rule induction. Section 5 introduces the Arabic-English transfer rules induction technique. Section 6 reports results from rule-based translation experiments that use induced rules from a relatively small data set. Section 7 gives some concluding remarks with direction for future work.

2. Inductive Logic Programming

Inductive Logic Programming (ILP) (Muggleton 1999) is a machine learning approach that uses logic programming as a representation for examples, background knowledge, and hypotheses. Given an encoding of the known background knowledge and a set of examples represented as a logical database of facts, an ILP system derives a hypothesized logic program which entails all the positive and none of the negative examples.

ILP works in three steps: (1) analyze input and output data according to the previous experience of the subject to get some kind of abstraction on both source and target in order to be mapped later, (2) train the system positively to identify which input should be mapped to which output as logical production rules, and (3) train the system negatively to identify which inputs should never map to which output.

The use of ILP in natural language processing (NLP) requires that we recognize the structure of the sentence and its linguistic features (i.e. feature structures representing the linguistic knowledge of each word). Then, this information is used in the unification between the left-hand and right-hand sides of the induced rule. The system should be trained positively on a valid set of input-output example pairs. The system also should be trained negatively on a set of non-valid example pairs in order to induce the negative rules that will act as excluding rules. Negative training for NLP tasks is hard as there is usually an infinite number of language combinations that do not match on the lexical, morphological, syntactic and semantic level.

The main advantage of ILP, in general, is that it provides logarithmic growth for first order learning (Dans 2005). This leads to degradation of newly generated rules after a limited set of trainings. ILP has been successfully implemented in NLP tasks like morphological analysis (Hossny et al. 2008), Part of Speech (POS) tagging (Eineborg et al. 1999), POS disambiguation (Lindberg et al. 1999), and machine translation (Hossny et al. 2009). In this paper, we address exploiting ILP to automatically induce Arabic-to-English rules from chunks of parallel linguistic resources.

3. Hybrid machine translation systems

Our focus is on the development of a hybrid machine translation system. The system is based on an Arabic-to-English rule-based machine translation approach that uses induced rules in its transfer and analysis steps. An example-based machine learning approach, which is the main contribution of the work presented here, is used to induce the Arabic-to-English transfer rules from a set of example pairs.

In the rest of this section, we briefly describe the notable hybrid machine translation systems for various languages that were developed from rule-based machine translation (RBMT), example-based machine translation (EBMT), and statistical-based machine translation (SMT) approaches.

3.1 RBMT/EBMT hybrids

Shirai et al. (1997) have proposed a method that gathers points of strength in both of RBMT and EBMT for English-Japanese Translation. The algorithm was briefly described in three steps (1) Select a set of candidate sentences which are similar to the input sentence, (2) Select the most typical translation out of those corresponding to the candidates, and (3) Use this translation and its source as templates to translate the input sentence. By discarding candidates with a typical translation, the algorithm filters out free, incorrect or context dependent translations.

Carl et al. (1998) described an NLP example-based translation application called Case-Based Analysis and Generation Module (CBAG), which is applied within a conventional RBMT system to drastically improve its performance. The main idea behind the CBAG module is to introduce a significant share of human translation experience accumulated in Translation Memories, which are, after all, relatively simple but very large and accurate collections of bilingual texts. They applied this application on English-French and English-German translation, and they could determine the types of word combinations, and chunks, introduced into a set of cases, that have a positive and sizeable effect on the translation quality and performance, and they could state the induction mechanisms to be used to extend the set of cases without creating additional noise.

3.2 RBMT/SMT hybrids

Ambati et al. (2007) have presented a hybrid EBMT/SMT approach to perform translation from English to Hindi. They performed matching by considering the longest match of the input sentence available in the example database, and performed the alignment using a manual and a statistical dictionary built from GIZA++ and the best Viterbi alignment given by GIZA++ for each sentence pair in the example database. Finally, the combination is done simply by merging different translated fragments to obtain the complete translated sentence.

Chen et al. (2007) have proposed an architecture that allows combining SMT with RBMT in a multi-engine setup. It uses a variant of standard SMT technology to align translations from one or more RBMT systems with the source text. They incorporated phrases extracted from these alignments into the phrase table of the SMT system and used the open-source decoder MOSES to find good combinations of phrases from SMT training data with the phrases derived from RBMT.

3.3 EBMT/SMT hybrids

Imamura et al. (2004) proposed an EBMT method based on syntactic transfer which selects the best translation by using models of SMT. The method proposed in this research selects the best translation by using a language model and a translation model in the same manner as SMT, and has proved that it can improve MT quality over that of 'pure' EBMT. The word re-ordering is achieved by syntactic transfer before applying the statistical models. This method improves both the MT quality and speed.

Sumita et al. (2004) conducted a project called Corpus-Centered Computation (C3). C3 places corpora at the center of its technology. Translation knowledge is extracted from corpora. Translation quality is gauged by referring to corpora; the best translation among multiple-engine outputs is selected based on corpora. The corpora themselves are paraphrased or filtered by automated processes to improve the data quality on which translation engines are based. This proposes two endeavors that are independent: (1) a hybridization of EBMT and statistical models, and (2) a new approach for SMT, phrase-based Hidden Markov Model (HMM). The hybridization was used in the "unrestricted" Japanese-to-English track while the phrase-based HMM was used in the "supplied" Japanese-to-English and Chinese-to-English tracks.

Aramaki et al. (2005) proposed a probabilistic language model, which deals with both the example size and the context similarity. The conducted experiments show that the proposed model has achieved a slightly better translation quality than the state-of-the-art EBMT systems. The proposed algorithm consists of two modules: alignment and translation modules. The alignment module builds translation examples from a corpus in three steps: (1) conversion into phrasal dependency structures, (2) alignment of phrases using a translation dictionary, and (3) building translation examples database. The translation module generates a translation through three steps: (1) input sentence analysis (2) select the closed translation examples, and (3) target sentence generation.

4. Related work

In this section, we briefly describe the related research on automatic rule induction from a data set of example pairs using different techniques for various languages.

4.1 A bootstrapping, template-driven approach to Example-Based MT

Veale et al. (1997) built a system, so-called Gaijin, which implements a template-driven approach to example-based English-German machine translation. Gaijin is a system that employs statistical methods, string-matching, case-based reasoning and template-matching to provide a linguistics-lite EBMT solution. The only lingual input needed by this system is psycholinguistic constraint – the marker hypothesis – that is minimal in size and simple to apply. The system consists of six sequential steps: (1) bilingual corpora alignment, (2) automatic lexical construction, (3) transfer-template generation, (4) example retrieval, (5) example adaptation, and (6) new example acquisition. The system generates template matching rule mapping from source to target as follows:

```
Template (24, English, German,
[s(A, prep, a24), s(B, det, b24), s(C, prep, c24), s(D, pro, d24),s(E, prep, e24) ],
[t(A, _, a24), t(B, det, b24), t(C, prep, c24), t([D|E], prep, [d24,e24])]).
```

4.2 Example-Based Machine Translation of the Basque language

Stroppa et al. (2006) presented a Data-Driven machine translation system which exploits both EBMT and SMT techniques to extract a data set of aligned (Basque-English) chunks. For the extraction of the EBMT data resources, they made use of two different chunking methods. In the case of English, they employed a marker-based chunker that depends on the marker hypothesis (Green 1979). For Basque, they used the dedicated tools developed at the University of the Basque Country while investigating the application of the marker-based chunker to Basque. The chunks are then aligned using a dynamic programming algorithm which is similar to an edit-distance algorithm while allowing for block movements (Leusch et al. 2006). This aligner also relies on relationships between chunks, which they compute in several ways.

4.3 Learning transfer rules for machine translation from limited data

Lavie et al. (2004) proposed a machine translation approach that is specifically designed to enable rapid development of machine translation for languages with limited amounts of online resources. Their approach assumes the availability of a small number of bi-lingual speakers of the two languages, but these need not be linguistic experts. The bi-lingual speakers create a comparatively small corpus of word aligned phrases and sentences (on the order of magnitude of a few thousand sentence pairs) using a specially designed elicitation tool. From this data, the learning module of the system automatically infers hierarchical syntactic transfer rules, which encode how syntactic constituent structures in the source language transfer to the target language (Probst et al. 2002). The collection of transfer rules is then used in the run-time system to translate previously unseen source language text into the target language. The reported results have significantly outperformed a SMT system on Hindi-to-English machine translation.

5. An Arabic-English transfer rules induction technique

In this section, we describe our experience on how we successfully constructed a rule-based translation model using inductive logic programming (ILP) (Muggleton 1999) to learn and induce Arabic-to-English transfer rules from chunks of the Linguistic Data Consortium's (LDC) parallel corpus (Arabic Treebank with English translation-LDC2005E46). The rule induction process consists of four main steps: (a) Word-to-Word alignment of sentence pairs extracted from the parallel corpus, (b) Partition each sentence into chunks, (c) Determine the patterns and feature structure representing the linguistic knowledge of each word using our morphological analysis tool, and (d) Induce translation rules by identifying, for each rule, the left-hand side (LHS) and the right-hand side (RHS) patterns and construct the link between them.

5.1 Word-to-word alignment

In order to exploit a parallel text, some kind of text alignment, which identifies equivalent text segments of source and target translations, is a prerequisite for rule induction. This step is similar to the alignment produced by Giza++ (Och et al. 2000). Figure 1 shows the word-to-word alignment of Example 1. It shows one-to-one and one-to-many word alignment.

Example 1: *Arabic-English word alignment of a parallel sentence*

Src. Indx	S1	S2	S3	S4	S5	S6	S7		
Src.	هزم	القطن	بطل	الكاميرون	من	الأهلي	المصري		
Align.	5, 6	4	3	1, 2	7	9	8		
Targt	The	Cameron's	champion	"Cotton"	was	defeated	by	Egyptian	Ahly
Targt Indx	T1	T2	T3	T4	T5	T6	T7	T8	T9
Translit.	huzima	Al.quT.nu	ɔaTal	Alka Amiyaruwn	min.	Al.Âah. liy~	Al.miS. riy		

We randomly selected 300 sentences from the LDC parallel corpus (LDC2005E46) in order to prove the capability of our machine learning approach in automating the induction of transfer rules from relatively small training data set of Arabic-English example pairs.

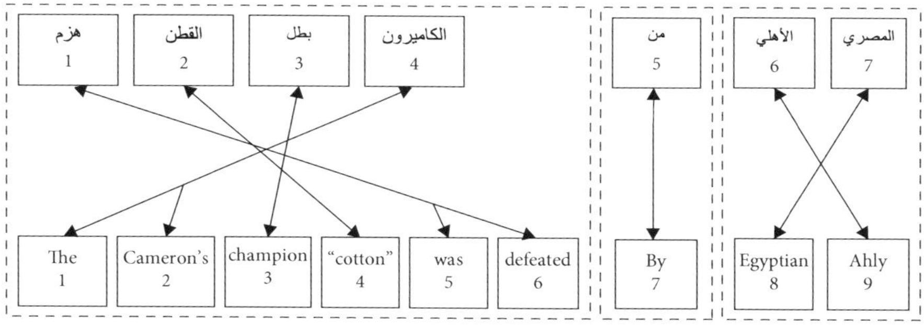

Figure 1. Arabic-English word alignment for a complex sentence leads to partitioning it to multiple chunks

5.2 Sentence partitioning

Sentence partitioning (chunking) is an important step in our induction process for two reasons: (1) It simplifies units used in induction by dealing with a phrase or chunk rather than an entire sentence which sometimes has a complex structure (Roh et al. 2001), and (2) induces a set of transfer rules per sentence instead of one which would result in a rich set of induced transfer rules with better coverage. These reasons have the impact of giving the transfer module of the intended machine translation system the opportunity to operate on rules at different granularity.

We perform partitioning of both the source and target sentence into a sequence of chunks based on word alignment dependency such that there is no overlap of word ordering between chunks. This is depicted in Figure 1. We used *Find Chunk Boundary* algorithm, see Figure 2, to detect the chunk boundaries, i.e. identify where we split the sentence into chunks, which is similar to the phrase extraction algorithm given by Koehn et al. (2003).

By applying the *Find Chunk Boundary* algorithm to Example 1, we get three chunks as shown in Figure 3. The identification of the first chunk is as follows. The algorithm starts by the source node S1, finds its target node T6, then traces backward the target sentence till its first node T1, and then finds its associated source node S4. It again traces backward the source sentence till the first node S1 of this chunk, i.e. the starting source node. This two-way process is repeated which results in two more chunks.

5.3 Arabic morphological analysis

Determining the morphological analysis by recognizing the feature structure representing the linguistic knowledge of each source word form is an important step before the actual induction of transfer rules takes place. The feature structure consists of a *feature:value* pair (e.g. gender:feminine, tense:perfect, and number:dual). During the course of transferring a source Arabic word into a target English word, these features might be carried over or modified, which affects the generation of the inflected forms of the target language.

We developed an Arabic morphological analyzer that applies morphological rules induced from monolingual parallel annotated example pairs. The morphologically induced rules are generated by our Automatic Morphological Rule Induction Tool (AMRIT). As shown in Figure 4, AMRIT induces morphological rules from monolingual example pairs of inflected forms and their stems.

The AMRIT module compares each example pair for their both vocal patterns and feature structure representations in order to induce the rule that causes the morphological changes. The vocal patterns are representations of the Arabic word consisting of a sequence of vowels and consonants (cf. Beesley 1996). An important feature of AMRIT is that it is able to automatically acquire both regular and irregular Arabic morphological analysis rules. Irregular forms, such as weak verbs and broken plurals, are very hard to analyze and marked correctly when tagging Arabic corpora. This is better explained by the following example:

```
Algorithm: Find Chunk Boundary
Input:    Ss: Source Sentence, Ts: Target Sentence, source_end: Source Chunk End Index,
          target_end: Target Chunk End Index
Parameters initial values:
          source_end = source chunk start position,
          target_end = target chunk start position,
Output: Index of the end of the chunk

  src_max_idx ← max (index of source_end)
  FOR each word target_word in target sentence Ts let target_idx be the index of target_word (where the target_idx is less than
  target_end)
          src_idx ← index (word associated with target_word in source sentence)
          IF Src_max_idx < src_idx THEN let Src_max_idx ← src_idx END IF
  END FOR
  target_end_word ← word at the target_end position in the target sentence Ts
  IF (src_max_idx > source_end) THEN
          let new_target_end ← FindChunkBoundary (Ts, Ss, target_end, src_max_id)
          IF new_target_end == target_end THEN
                  Return src_max_idx as the source chunk boundary.
          ELSE
                  Return new_src_idx as the index of the word associated with new_target_word in source sentence.
          END IF
  ELSE
          Return source_end
  END IF
```

Figure 2. An Algorithm for finding the chunk boundary from an aligned sentence pair

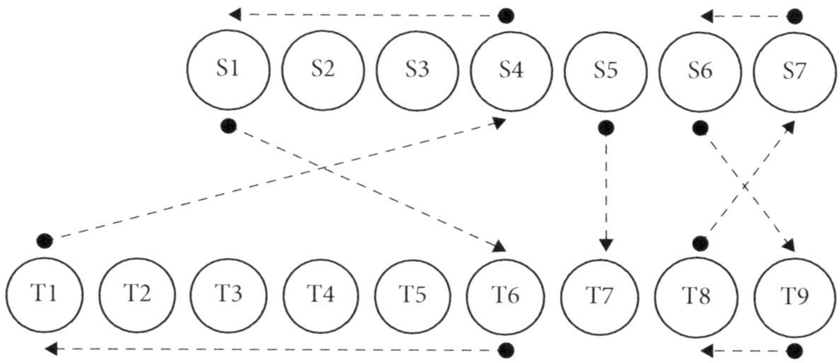

Figure 3. Two-way trace for detecting chunk boundaries for the three chunks

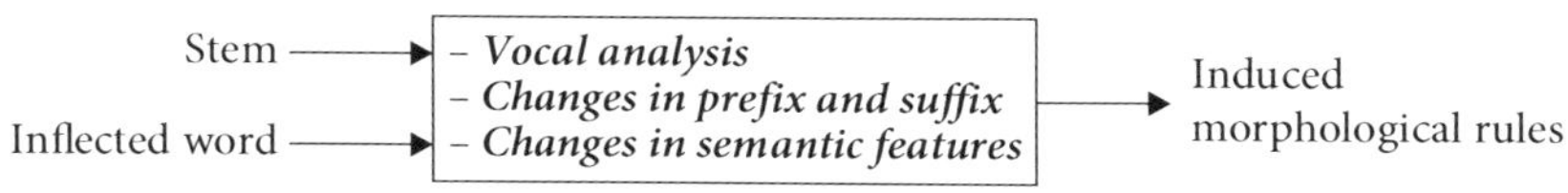

Figure 4. Morphological Rule induction process using AMRIT

Example 2: *A morphological analysis rule for analyzing the imperfect assimilated (weak initial radical) verb into its stem.*

Consider, the stem "وقى"/waqaý a/(to-protect) that has the vocal representation "VCV". In imperfect form, it becomes "يقى"/yaqiy./that is produced by removing the first weak radical letter "و" (Waw) and adding the imperfect tense prefix letter "ي" (Yeh). The induced rule that is generated by AMRIT from these two words is as follows:

> يقى → وقي
> *V2C1 ي (tense:imperfect) → V2C1 و (tense:perfect)*
> where V stands for vowels and C stands for consonants

Applying this rule by our Arabic morphological analyzer to analyze the imperfect form "يعى"/yaçiy./(is-conscious), which has the vocal representation (VC ى), yields the stem "وعى"/waçaýa/(to-be conscious), which has the vocal representation (VCو). Moreover, AMRIT is able to induce complex rules, e.g. the following rule analyzes the word 'يهتدون'/yah.taduw.n/(discover-/guide-they [pl,imperfect,masculine]) into the stem 'إهتدى'/ Ăih.tadaý/(discovered-/guided-he [sg, perfect, masculine]).

> *ونC3C2C1ي (tense:imperfect, gender:Masculine, number:plural, person:Third)*
> *→ ى+ونC3 C2 C1 ! (tense:perfect,gender:Masculine,number:singular,person: Third)+ي*

To demonstrate the capability of our Arabic morphological analyzer in analyzing a sentence using induced rules by AMRIT, consider the verbal sentence

"تقتدي الفرق بالأبطال"/taq.tadiy Al.far.qu biAlÂab.TaAl/(the teams take the champions as role model). The verb "تقتدي"/taq.tadiy/(take-as-role-module – an imperfect form of the stem إقتدى/Ăiq.tadaý/) will be analyzed exactly in a way similar to the verb "يهتدي"/yah.tadiy/. The noun "الفرق"/Al.far.q/(teams – a broken plural of the noun فرقة/fir.qaħ/) will be analyzed exactly in a way similar to the noun "البرك"/Al.bir~ak/(bonds – a broken plural of the noun "بركة"/barakaħ/). The noun "الأبطال"/Al.Âab.TaAl/(champions – a broken plural of the noun "بطل"/baTal/) will be analyzed exactly in a way similar to the noun "الأعطال"/Al.Âaç.TaAl/(malfunctions – a broken plural of the noun "عطل"/çuTil/).

To sum up, our Arabic morphological analyzer uses the induced rules to analyze each word in the input Arabic sentence to generate its stem and feature structure representing the linguistic knowledge of this word. This results in a representation suitable for rule induction which consists of a sequence of chunks, each of which consists of a sequence of morphologically analyzed words with their linguistic features.

5.4 Transfer rule induction

5.4.1 *Rule construction*

The transfer rule construction process involves establishing a mapping from a sequence of source chunks (LHS) to a sequence of target chunks (RHS). We recall that a chunk itself is a sequence of words. Each word is represented by a feature structure that encodes its linguistic knowledge. So, a transfer rule maps the source linguistic knowledge into a target linguistic knowledge.

The rule construction process considers the induction of rules at varying grain size in order to allow for selecting the applicable rule that matches the input pattern. This gives the induced transfer rules better coverage. In the following, we show how transfer rules are induced from chunks shown in Figure 1.

So far, we have three source chunks [S1 + S2 + S3 + S4], [S5] and [S6 + S7] linked with three target chunks [T1 + T2 + T3 + T4 + T5 + T6], [T7] and [T8 + T9], respectively. As shown in Figure 5, these chunks can be used to generate six induced rules: (1) one rule composed of a sequence of three chunks, (2) two rules composed of a sequence of two chunks, and (3) three rules composed of a sequence of one chunk. In general, the number of rules generated per source sentence is the sum of a number series 1 to n, where n is the number of chunks generated from this sentence:

$$\sum_{i=0}^{n} i = 1 + 2 + \ldots + n = \left(n * \left(n+1\right)\right) / 2$$

1 rule with 3 chunks:
Rule1: [S1 + S2 + S3 + S4] + [S5] + [S6 + S7] → [T1 + T2 + T3 + T4 + T5 + T6] + [T7] +[T8 + T9]

2 rules with 2 chunks each:
Rule2: [S1 + S2 + S3 + S4] + [S5] → [T1 + T2 + T3 + T4 + T5 + T6] + [T7]
Rule3: [S5] + [S6 + S7] → [T7] + [T8 + T9]

3 rules with 1 chunk each:
Rule4: [S1 + S2 + S3 + S4] → [T1 + T2 + T3 + T4 + T5 + T6]
Rule5: [S5] → [T7]
Rule6: [S6 + S7] → [T8 + T9]

Figure 5. Three chunks can generate up to six induced rules

Each term *i* in this series forms a group of rules consisting of i rules, each of which links a sequence of source *i* chunks with a sequence of target *i* chunks.

5.4.2 *Feature Unification*

After the rule structure is determined, the *feature:value* pairs of each word in both sides (Arabic–English) of the induced rule is unified using Unification Based Grammar formalism. This unification process will result in setting specific feature value constraint (a constant represented by symbols that has initial lower case letter), determining a variable to be unified during the machine translation process (represented by an identifier with an initial upper case letter) in order to apply carried over source linguistic constraint, and generating anonymous variable (underscore symbol to suppress irrelevant value). For example, consider the following transfer rule:

> *{number:S1,gender:masc, cat:verb, tense:P1} → {number:S1, gender:_, cat:verb, tense:P1}*

This rule says that in order to transfer a source Arabic verb into a target English verb, the *gender* of the source verb should be set to *masculine*, and both source and target verbs should be mapped to the same *number* and *tense*. Notice that the gender of the English verb is neither constrained to a specific value nor carried over. So, it is set to anonymous value.

5.5 An example of a transfer rule induction

In this section, we give an example of a transfer rule induction. The steps specified above are applied on an aligned Arabic-English chunk pair to induce the rule shown in Figure 6. Then, we demonstrate how the induced rule can be used by the transfer module of a machine translation system to transfer a similar source Arabic input into a target English output.

Chunk 1 = هزم الأهلي المصري
Chunk 2 = The Egyptian al-Ahly defeated

Arabic-English word alignment:
هزم + الأهلي + المصري → The Egyptian + al-Ahly + defeated
Wa[1] + Wa[2] + Wa[3] → The We[3] + We[2] + We[1]

Arabic morphological analysis:
هزم (Wa[1]) {number:singular, gender:masc, cat:verb, tense:perfect}
Defeated (We [1]) {number:singular, gender:masc, cat:verb, tense:perfect}

الأهلي (Wa[2]) {number:singular, gender:_, sub_cat:propernoun}
al-Ahly (We[2]) {number:singular, gender:_, sub_cat:propernoun}

المصري (Wa[3]) {number:singular, gender:masc, sub_cat:adj, definite_article:yes}
The {definite_article:yes}
Egyptian (We[3]) {number:singular, gender:masc, sub_cat:adj}

Constructing an inductive rule:
Wa[1] {number:singular, gender:masc, cat:verb, tense:perfect} +
Wa[2] {number:singular, gender:_, sub_cat:propernoun} +
Wa[3] {number:singular, gender:masc, sub_cat:adjective, definite_article:yes} →
The {definite_article:yes} +
We[3] {number:singular, gender:masc, sub_cat:adj} +
We[2] {number:singular, gender:_, sub_cat:propernoun} +
We[1] {number:singular, gender:masc, cat:verb, tense:perfect}

Unifying LHS & RHS sides of the inductive rule
Wa[1] {number:S1, gender:masc, cat:verb, tense:P1} +
Wa[2] {number:S2, gender:_ , sub_cat:propernoun} +
Wa[3] {number:C3, gender:S3, sub_cat:T3, definite_article:yes} →
The {definite_article:yes} +
We[3] {number:C3, gender:_, sub_cat:T3} +
We[2] {number:S2, gender:_, sub_cat:propernoun} +
We[1] {number:S1, gender:_, cat:verb, tense:P1}

Figure 6. An example of constructing Arabic-English transfer rule from an aligned chunk

Figure 7 shows the results of applying the transfer rule induced in Figure 6 to the first aligned chunk of the source Arabic sentence "حققت فينوس البطلة رقم قياسي جديد" /Haq~aqt fiy.nuws Al.baTalah raq.m qiyaAsiy jadiy.d/ in order to transfer it to a format suitable for generating the target English sentence.

Arabic Sentence = حققت فينوس البطلة رقم قياسي جديد
English Sentence = [The champion Venus achieved new record]

Sentence partitioning:
Chunk1 = حققت فينوس البطلة → The champion Venus achieved
Chunk2 = رقم قياسي جديد → new record

Arabic-English word alignment:
حققت + فينوس + البطلة → The champion + Venus + achieved
Wa[1] + Wa[2] + Wa[3] → The We[3] + We[2] + We[1]

Arabic Morphological analysis:

حققت	(Wa[1])	{number:singular, gender:fem, cat:verb, tense:perfect}
فينوس	(Wa[2])	{number:singular, gender:fem, sub_cat:propernoun}
البطلة	(Wa[3])	{number:singular, gender:fem, sub_cat:adj, definite_article:yes}

Matching with the induced rule:

Wa[1]	{number:S1, gender:masc, cat:verb, tense:P1}	+
Wa[2]	{number:S2, gender:_, sub_cat:propernoun}	+
Wa[3]	{number:C3, gender:S3, sub_cat:T3, definite_article:yes}	
→		
The	{definite_article:yes}	+
We[3]	{number:C3, gender: _, sub_cat:T3}	+
We[2]	{number:S2, gender:_, sub_cat:propernoun}	+
We[1]	{number:S1, gender:_, cat:verb, tense:P1}	

Transfer output:

The	{definite_article:yes}
We[3] = champion	{number:singular, gender:_, sub_cat:adj}
We[2] = Venus	{number:singular, gender:_, sub_cat:propernoun}
We[1] = Achieved	{number:singular, gender:_, cat:verb, tense:perfect}

Figure 7. An example of applying Arabic-English induced transfer rule

6. Experiments

To evaluate our inductive machine learning technique, we conducted two related experiments using considerably small dataset. The objective of the first experiment is to measure the effect of the number of training examples on Arabic-English transfer rule induction. The objective of the second evaluation experiment is to assess the translation performance by comparing the automatically translated sentences with a gold standard reference test data. Figure 8 shows an illustration of the scheme used to conduct these two experiments.

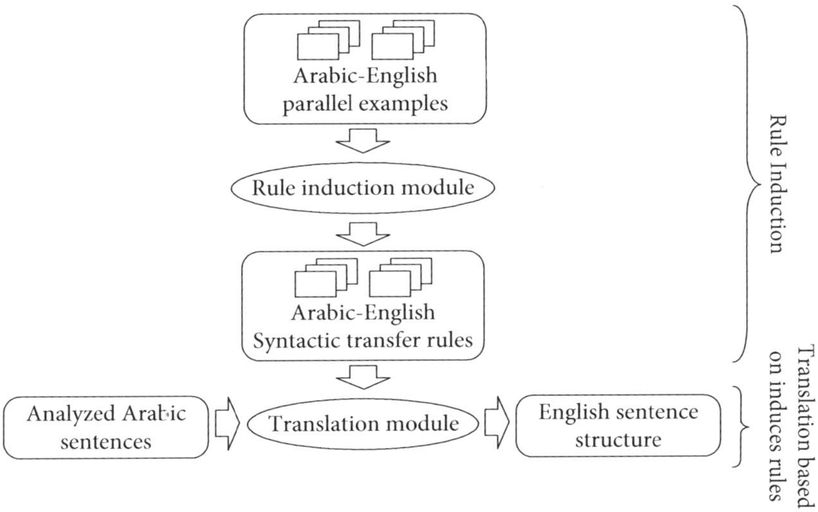

Figure 8. Experiments to evaluate two modules: rule induction and machine translation module built on top of it

6.1 Rule induction experiment

A set of 300 parallel sentences was used as a test set. The average sentence length is 10 words. This set was randomly chosen from the Arabic Treebank with English translation (LDC2005E46). We applied our sentence partitioning (chunking) algorithm on the 300 parallel aligned examples, which produced 2087 chunks with the frequency distribution of 1 to 10 chunk size shown in Table 1.

Table 1. Frequency distribution of chunks

Chunk size	1	2	3	4	5	6–7	8–10	**Total**
Frequency	1498	304	151	81	32	15	6	2087

The rule induction of these chunks has produced 1115 unique Arabic-to-English transfer rules. Figure 9 shows that the growth rate of the number of induced rules proportional to the number of chunks takes a logarithmic shape. This observation indicates that our induction technique is capable of inducing from a relatively small dataset the most frequently used Arabic-to-English transfer rules.

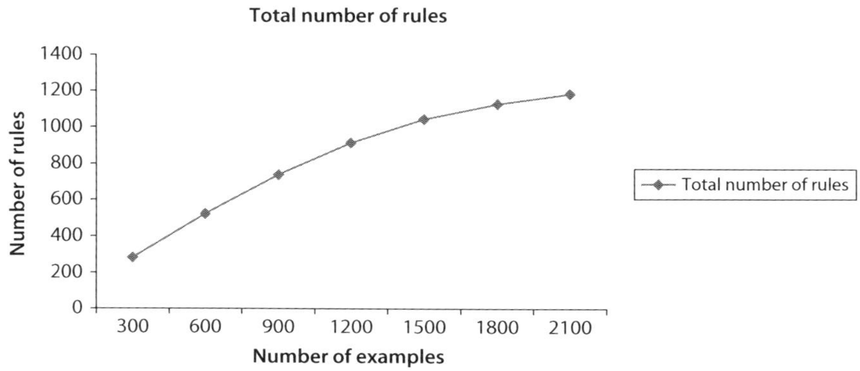

Figure 9. Growth rate of the total number of induced rules

The analysis of results has shown that the higher similarity of the induced rules the lower the newly induced rules and the vice versa. In our experiment, we found that there are two factors affecting the similarity of newly induced rules: Part of speech (POS) and chunk size. As the number of POS's increases, the probability of rules similarity decreases. Moreover, increasing the number of words in a chunk leads to a lower probability of similarity.

6.2 Translation performance experiment

A second experiment that uses another 180 dataset from LDC2005E46 is conducted. The objective is to test the performance of a hybrid rule-based Arabic-English machine translation system that is built on top of the induced syntactic transfer rules produced by the previous experiment. We employed Word Error Rate (WER) metric which has been used in evaluating machine translation when the word sequence output can have a different length from the reference word sequence. The results depend on the minimum chunk size (i.e. rule size) and the sentence size (number of rules used in the translation process). Table 2 shows the effect of chunk size on both coverage and error rate. From this table we observe that the minimum chunk size is in a reverse proportion both the coverage and error ratio.

Table 2. The effect of chunk size on coverage and error rate

Minimum chunk size	Coverage	Error rate
1	100%	88%
2	96%	68%
3	80%	39%
4	54%	24%
5	23%	11%

7. Conclusion and future work

In this chapter, we described exploiting a supervised machine learning technique to develop a novel example-based transfer tool that automatically induce Arabic-to-English transfer rules from chunks of relatively small aligned parallel linguistic resources. This tool is very important for those who would like to do Arabic machine translation research but find that the parallel linguistic resources for their translation task are neither available nor affordable. Low density Arabic Script languages like Pashto/Farsi/Amharic can also benefit from the rule induction approach in building their transfer-based machine translation systems.

During the course of rule induction a morphological analysis process is needed, which entails the acquisition of linguistic knowledge. Again, the role of supervised machine learning technique comes into play in order to develop a novel morphological acquisition tool that incrementally acquires induced morphological rules. The rules are induced from a set of monolingual example pairs of inflected forms and their stems based on their vocal patterns and feature structure. This tool is very important for a morphologically rich language like Arabic as it automates the acquisition of morphological rules from examples rather than relying on hand-crafted linguistic rules acquired from Arabic specialists.

This research discusses how to build from a relatively small aligned parallel data set a machine translation system that can make use of induced Arabic-to-English syntactic transfer rules. Although much work has shown that large amount of data can successfully be used to build a machine translation system, we still need to prove that with small amounts of data we can also successfully build a machine translation system. For example, domain-specific machine translation systems usually do not require large amount of data to get acceptable translations.

To demonstrate the capability of this automated technique we conducted rule-based translation experiments that use induced rules from a relatively small dataset. The rule induction experiment achieved a negative exponential growth of the newly induced rules by increasing the number of the training examples which leads to saturation of the transfer rules after a specific number of examples. The translation quality experiment achieved good results in terms of both coverage and quality.

Much remains to be done in the field of rule induction in the context of machine translation. One possible future direction is to reduce the tradeoff between coverage and quality of translation rules. Another direction is to investigate how to apply statistical weights on the induced rules to resolve possible ambiguities.

References

Abdel Monem, A., K. Shaalan, A. Rafea, and H. Baraka. 2008. Generating Arabic text in multilingual speech-to-speech machine translation framework. *Machine Translation* 20 (4): 205–258.

Ambati, V., and U. Rohini. 2007. A hybrid approach to example based machine translation for Indian languages. In *ICON-2007: 5th International Conference on Natural Language Processing*, IIIT Hyderabad, India.

Aramaki, E., S. Kurohashi, H. Kashioka, and N. Kato. 2005. Probabilistic model for example-based machine translation. *In Proceedings of MT Summit X*, 219–226. Phuket, Thailand

Beesley, K. 1996. Arabic finite state morphological analysis and generation. *In Proceedings of the 16th Conference on Computational Linguistics*, 89–94

Carl, M., C. Pease, L. Iomdin, and O. Streiter. 1998. Towards dynamic linkage of example based and rule-based machine translation. *In Proceedings of ESSLLI '98 Machine Translation Workshop*.

Chen, Y., A. Eisele, C. Federmann, E. Hasler, M. Jellinghaus, and S. Theison. 2007. Multi-engine machine translation with an open-source decoder for statistical machine translation. *In Proceedings of Association of Computational Linguistics* (ACL 2007).

Dans, K. 2005. Online closure based learning of relational theories. *In ILP'05:* Inductive Logic Programming, 172–189, Bonn, Germany,

Eineborg, M., and N. Lindberg. 1999. ILP in part of speech tagging – an overview. in *Learning Language in Logic*, 57–169.

Green, T. 1979. The necessity of syntax markers, two experiments with artificial languages. *Journal of Verbal Learning and Behaviour* 18(4): 481–496.

Hossny, A., K. Shaalan, A. Fahmy, 2009. Machine translation model using inductive logic programming. In *Proceedings of IEEE international conference on natural language processing and knowledge engineering (IEEE NLP-KE'09)*, 103–110. Dalian, China.

Imamura, K., H. Okuma, T. Watanabe, and E. Sumita. 2004. Example-based machine translation based on syntactic transfer with statistical models. In *Proceedings of the 20th International Conference on Computational Linguistics, 99–105.* Geneva.

Koehn, P., F. Och, and D. Marcu. 2003. Statistical phrase-based translation. In *Proceedings of the Joint Human Language Technology Conference and the Annual Meeting of the North American Chapter of the Association for Computational Linguistics (HLT-NAACL)*, 127–133. Edmonton, Canada.

Lavie, A., K. Probst, E. Peterson, S. Vogel, L. Levin, A. Font-Llitjos, and J. Carbonell. 2004. A trainable transfer-based MT approach for languages with limited resources. In *Proceedings of Workshop of the European Association for Machine Translation* (EAMT-2004), 116–123.Valletta, Malta.

Leusch, G., N. Ueffing, and H. Ney. 2006. CDER: efficient MT evaluation using block movements. In *Proceedings of the 11th Conference of the European Chapter of the Association for Computational Linguistics*, 241–248

Lindberg, N., and M. Eineborg. 1999. Improving part of speech disambiguation rules by adding linguistic knowledge. *ILP*: 186–197.

Muggleton, S. 1999. Inductive logic programming issues, results and the challenge of learning language in logic. *Artificial Intelligence* 114 (1–2): 283–296.

Och, F., and H. Ney. 2000. Improved statistical alignment models. In *Proceeding of the 38th Annual Meeting of the Association for Computational Linguistics*, 440–447. Hongkong, China.

Probst, K., L. Levin, E. Peterson, A. Lavie, and J. Carbonell. 2002. Machine translation for minority languages using elicitation based learning of syntactic transfer rules. *Machine Translation* 17 (4): 245–270.

Riezler, S., and J Maxwell. 2006. Grammatical machine translation. In *Proceedings of HLT-NAACL '06 Proceedings of the main conference on Human Language Technology Conference of the North American Chapter of the Association of Computational Linguistics, Association for Computational Linguistics, Stroudsburg, PA, USA*, 248–255.

Shirai, S., F. Bond, and Y. Takahashi. 1997. A hybrid rule and example-based method for machine translation. In *Proceedings of the Natural Language Processing Pacific Rim Symposium*, 49–54. Phuket, Thailand.

Stroppa, N., D. Groves, A. Way, and K. Sarasola. 2006. Example based machine translation of the Basque language. In *Proceedings of the 7th biennial conference of the Association for Machine Translation in the Americas*, 232–241, Cambridge MA.

Sumita, E., Y. Akiba, T. Doi, A. Finch, K. Imamura, H. Okuma, M. Paul, M. Shimohata, & T. Watanabe, 2004. EBMT, SMT, Hybrid and More: ATR spoken language translation system. In Proceeding of International Workshop on Spoken Language Translation, 13–20. Kyoto, Japan.

Veale, T., and A. Way. 1997. Gaijin: A bootstrapping, template-driven approach to example-based machine translation. In *Proceedings of the New Methods in Natural Language Processing (NeMNLP97)*, 239–244. Sofia, Bulgaria.

Yoon-Hyung Roh, Young Ae Seo, Ki-Young Lee, Sung-Kwon Choi. 2001. Long Sentence Partitioning using Structure Analysis for Machine Translation. Proceedings of the Sixth Natural Language Processing Pacific Rim Symposium, Tokyo, Japan.

Index

A
adaptation 23, 26–27, 35, 38, 109, 140
align 63, 100, 139, 141
aligning 7, 68
alignment 19–21, 34, 40, 44, 55, 63, 65, 68, 75–76, 84, 101, 104, 111, 138–142
ambiguity 1, 4–5, 9, 27, 30, 32, 35–36, 45, 47, 56, 77–79, 97, 109, 112, 132
disambiguation 7, 59, 73–76, 79–81, 91, 137
arabic VII, VIII, 1–12, 15–21, 23–24, 26–30, 34, 36–42, 44–47, 49–60, 62–69, 73–86, 91, 95–106, 109, 111, 117, 121, 125–126, 130, 135–138, 141–151
machine translation VII, VIII, 1–10, 15–21, 23–25, 52–54, 65, 68–69, 73, 95–96, 98–99, 106, 109, 121, 123, 135–138, 140–142, 146–147, 149–151
analysis VII, 2–8, 10, 18, 27–28, 30–31, 33, 36–38, 45, 73–75, 78–80, 86, 91, 96, 116, 119, 131, 135–139, 141, 143–144, 150–151
syntax 2, 5, 9–10, 54, 62–63, 73–74, 83, 96, 99, 101, 106, 109–116, 121–122, 124, 126, 136
syntactic reordering VII, 9, 95, 99–101, 103–105
rewrite rules 39–40, 46–47
multiple analyses 28–30, 32, 45, 80
treebank 5, 18–21, 38, 75, 77, 80, 82, 84, 141, 149
morphology 1–4, 23, 26–27, 42–45, 56, 74, 79–80, 106, 136
language VII, 1–5, 8–10, 15–16, 19–20, 23, 25–27, 30, 34, 38, 42, 44, 46–47, 50–54, 59, 62–63, 66, 68, 73–77, 83–84, 88, 95, 97–101, 104–105, 109–110, 116–122, 124–125, 127, 129–130, 132, 136–137, 139–141, 143, 151
stem 2, 6–9, 18, 28–31, 33, 44, 50–51, 53, 55–58, 60, 63–64, 75, 82, 96–99, 144–145
stemmed word 31
diacritic 4, 18, 27–28, 77
semantics 2, 113–114

B
buckwalter morphological analyzer 6, 55–56, 60, 63
bama 5, 18, 28–32, 36, 38–39, 79–81, 85–87
bleu 43, 46, 60–61, 66–68, 73–74, 76, 84–91, 98–99, 104–105, 118–119, 130–131
bleu score 60, 68, 73–74, 76, 84, 86, 88–91, 104, 118–119, 131

C
canonical stem 30
chart 34, 110
clitic 39, 78, 82
decliticization 82
cluster 31, 33–34, 36, 38
clustering 31–32, 34–38, 44
clusters 31–34, 36, 38, 44, 46
context-insensitive 28, 32
corpus 2–8, 10, 16, 20–21, 24–27, 29–34, 36, 38–42, 44–46, 49–55, 59–63, 65, 67–69, 75, 79, 83–85, 88, 98–99, 104–105, 110, 116–118, 125–126, 130, 135–136, 139–142
parallel corpus 7–8, 24, 26, 44, 49–54, 60, 62, 75, 83–84, 110, 116–118, 125–126, 130, 136, 141–142
training corpus 2, 8, 24, 29, 33, 41, 46, 51, 79, 84–85, 98–99, 117
un arabic-english parallel text 41
coverage 2, 18–19, 24, 26, 31–32, 34, 39, 46, 49–51, 61, 109–110, 136, 142, 145, 150–151

F
filtering 25, 27, 30, 32–35, 38

G
generalization 27–36, 38–47, 112
generalize 4, 6, 10, 27, 30, 40, 44–45, 55
generalizing 23, 29–31, 34–35, 44–46
genre 19–20, 42, 73–74, 76, 85, 87, 91
graph clustering 36

H
hallucinations 34
hybrid 2, 10, 26, 135–138, 150
hybridization 23, 139

I
inductive 3, 10, 136–137, 141, 148
inductive logic programming 3, 136–137, 141
transfer rule induction 145–146, 148

L
language VII, 1–5, 8–10, 15–16, 19–20, 23, 25–27, 30, 34, 38, 42, 44, 46–47, 50–54, 59, 62–63, 66, 68, 73–77, 83–84, 88, 95, 97–101, 104–105, 109–110, 116–122, 124–125, 127, 129–130, 132, 136–137, 139–141, 143, 151
model 2, 4, 6–10, 15–16, 23, 25, 42, 45, 59, 68, 76, 83–84, 87–88, 96–98, 100–101, 104–105, 109–110, 112, 116–118, 120–122, 124–127, 129–132, 135, 139, 141, 145
models 2, 5, 25–26, 55, 76, 84, 99–100, 109–110, 116–117, 119, 121, 125–126, 130, 139
lm 34–35, 38–39, 43, 46, 105, 118
resources VII, 2–3, 5, 7, 15–17, 19–21, 74–75, 79, 85, 135–137, 140, 151
LDC Arabic Treebank
treebanks 18–21, 86, 111
ldc 3, 5, 7, 15–21, 38, 84, 98, 104, 117, 130, 141–142
lemmatization 73, 75
lemmaid 28–32, 35–38
lexicalized tree adjoining grammars 10

M
match 2, 6, 8, 27, 29, 32–34, 38–40, 49–50, 52, 55–57, 59–60, 63–64, 68, 89, 99–101, 115, 131, 137–138
matching 6–8, 25, 31, 38, 44, 46–47, 50–55, 57, 59–64, 66–68, 76, 79, 96, 138, 140
mcl toolkit 38
memt
metadata 29–30, 33, 46
morphological VII, 1–10, 18–19, 21, 23, 27–32, 34–47, 51–57, 59–60, 63, 73–80, 83, 86, 91, 95–99, 126, 135–137, 141, 143–145, 151
analysis VII, 2–8, 10, 18, 27–28, 30–31, 33, 36–38, 45, 73–75, 78–80, 86, 91, 96, 116, 119, 131, 135–139, 141, 143–144, 150–151
analyzer 5–6, 8, 18, 28, 30, 38, 51, 55–56, 59–60, 63, 78–79, 81, 96, 135–136, 143–145
features 6, 10, 27–28, 32, 35, 38–41, 44–46, 52, 56, 60, 62–64, 66, 69, 75, 77–80, 83, 88–89, 113, 115, 125–127, 130, 137, 143, 145
rule induction 135–136, 140–141, 143–146, 148–149, 151
segmentation 3, 8–9, 45, 75–76, 95–96, 98–99, 126
variant 77, 86, 139
variants 27, 30–31, 34, 77–78, 81, 112, 129
morphology 1–4, 23, 26–27, 42–45, 56, 74, 79–80, 106, 136
part-of-speech 18, 44, 55–56, 64, 73–74, 80, 91, 103, 126
segmentation 3, 8–9, 45, 75–76, 95–96, 98–99, 126
supertagging 10, 114, 116–117, 120–121
affix 75, 96

N
nist 5, 17, 40, 42, 60, 67, 74, 83–85, 104–105, 117, 130
nistmt evaluation 40, 42, 60, 74, 85

O
out-of-vocabulary 83, 88, 96, 99, 131
overgeneralize 27, 38

P
parameter 63, 65, 98
perplexity 83, 88–89
preprocessing 8–9, 30, 45, 53–54, 73–82, 84, 86–89, 91, 95–96, 99–100, 105–106
preprocessing schemes 54, 73–74, 76, 79–81, 88–89, 91

S
score 40–44, 46, 52–53, 55–57, 59–60, 68, 73–74, 76, 84, 86–91, 104–105, 118–119, 131
scoring 17, 40–41, 46
statistical VII, 2–10, 23–26, 44–45, 49, 52–54, 59, 73, 79, 90, 95–96, 100, 106, 109, 116, 123, 135–136, 138–140, 151
surface form 4, 6, 29, 31, 33, 36, 46
synonyms 6–7, 44, 49–51, 53–63, 65–69

T
text collections 17
speech collections 16
tokenization 73–74, 76, 79–80, 82–83, 91
translation VII, VIII, 1–10, 15–21, 23–27, 33–35, 38–46, 49–63, 65–69, 73, 75–76, 84, 88, 95–96, 98–101, 104, 106, 109–110, 112, 116–126, 128–132, 135–142, 146–151
direct translation model 10, 110, 124–126
ebmt 23–26, 33–34, 38, 40, 43–46, 52, 68, 138–140
example-based VII, 2–7, 23–24, 45, 49–50, 52–54, 68, 136–138, 140, 151

Example-Based-Machine-Translation
knolwledge-based
multi-engine machine translation
multi-engine system 26
phrase-based statistical mt 10
phrase-based smt 73–74, 84, 100, 109–110, 132, 136
rule-based machine translation 24, 137–138
rbmt 24, 138–139
statistical machine transaltion
smt 23–26, 43, 45–46, 73–76, 79, 82–84, 86, 95–96, 99–101, 109–113, 116, 125, 132, 136, 138–141
probability 25, 38, 40, 53, 114, 116, 124–125, 150
transfer-based machine translation 3, 151
translation approach 137, 140
translation candidate 38
translation engine 135
translation quality 23, 34, 62, 75, 100, 109–110, 117–118, 132, 135, 138–139, 151
spurious translations 34
performance 6, 8, 25, 30, 35–36, 40–41, 43–44, 52, 61, 74, 84, 89, 91, 119, 130, 136, 138, 148, 150
incremental parsing for mt
data-driven 2, 4–6, 9, 24–26, 45, 140
empirical 2, 24, 135